GOD'S GRACE IN DIVORCE

CHOOSING BETWEEN PRESERVING THE MARRIAGE AND PROTECTING THE CHILDREN

ISIDOR BUCHMANN

WinePress WP Publishing

God's Grace in Divorce—Choosing Between Preserving the Marriage and Protecting the Children.

To protect privacy, the names of my wife, my children, and my friends have been changed.

ISBN 13: 978-1-57921-993-2
ISBN 10: 1-57921-993-4
Library of Congress Catalog Card Number: 2009922586

Dedicated to my beloved children

Who are witness to our family problems and contributed to this book with great enthusiasm. Together, we bring a message of endurance, love, and hope to families in crisis. With God's help, victory is at hand and we rise above the ashes.

This book is written for couples who are burdened with marital problems and are at a crossroad. I pray that these spouses and parents have the strength to walk the difficult road and make a decision that is best for the children.

"The supreme function of reason is to
show man that some things are beyond reason."

—Blaise Pascal

CONTENTS

AUTHOR'S COMMENT

When we marry and start a family, we carry with us the hope for a better world. We glance at the generation that has passed before us, see their failings, and resolve to do better. God appreciates our noble intentions, but He also places obstacles in our journey.

We often become victims of uncontrolled circumstances. We are tossed in a merciless sea, helpless and wondering what has brought on such a calamity. During times of stress, we must do what's best for our own good and that of the family. The path we choose may not always agree with established conventions. God understands the departure and blesses our actions if done in good faith and love.

God's Grace in Divorce—Choosing Between Preserving the Marriage and Protecting the Children serves as escort and friend when traveling on a difficult road alone. It is my deep desire to share the burden of a failed marriage with you to bring hope and healing. Together we conquer the disappointments and find new strength through God's enduring love. His outstretched arms will rescue us and guide our families to a calm harbor.

—Isidor Buchmann

The opinions expressed in this book are not from a theologian or psychiatrist, but reflect the experience of a father raising five children under troubled circumstances.

INTRODUCTION

Divorce can be a gift to a family . . . if it's done to save the children from a dysfunctional and dangerous family environment.

This is a shocking thesis to many readers, mainly to those with a Christian faith background, just as it has been a shocking discovery to me. It's not a statement that I had ever imagined I would make. As a committed, lifelong Christian, I had prayed for a devoted wife and family ever since I was a young boy growing up in Switzerland. As Catholics, we were promised the fulfillment of our wishes if we prayed 4,000 Hail Marys during Advent. That translated into 130 Hail Marys per day, and I dutifully performed the ritual, believing it was part of my preparation for a lifelong, gratified, and blessed marriage to a loving woman whom God would bring into my life.

Life rarely turns out as we expect, but even in my most fervent prayers, I could never have imagined that I would one day find myself contemplating divorce. Until the day of our separation, I had hoped that God would intervene and help save the marriage. But help never came, and despite twenty years of loving my wife, Sophie, I found myself living amidst circumstances that I could never have imagined. Her behavior had become increasingly erratic over the years, eventually resulting in her being diagnosed by psychiatrists as bipolar.

Such a diagnosis always commands our compassion toward the afflicted, but the words don't begin to convey the hurt and chaos that were inflicted on our family by the disease, and most of all, by her stubborn refusal to undergo any type of treatment.

Gradually, my growing family was subjected to inexplicable behavioral changes, including bouts of physical and verbal abuse, uncontrolled and lavish shopping sprees, and even the impulsive start of home renovation projects during her manic phases. For a time, "Sophie, the career woman" was transformed into "Sophie, the teenage rock star," who formed a rock-and-roll band and stayed out until the wee hours of the morning, ostensibly "practicing" and "rediscovering herself." But the turning point for her and our family finally came after a nervous breakdown, a dive into paranoia and the admission that she had experienced visions and heard "voices" speaking to her.

Her mental condition exposed a young family to uncertainty about how their mother would react. What she would do or say next was one thing, but it was her unyielding belief that I was an evil man with bad intentions, which compelled me to break my twenty-year marriage vow and accept her divorce petition. As a father of five children, I had no other choice than to remove her from the family and offer the children a more predictable home life.

As everything that I had treasured so deeply began falling apart, I reached a point where my convictions and beliefs became meaningless. The Bible, with its many promises and answers, began annoying me to no end. It didn't address mental disorders of a spouse or the problems inherent to a dysfunctional family caused by complex mental illness issues.

In my darkest hours, when I began realizing that the teachings of the Bible no longer made sense to me, I threw the book to the ground. I became empty, utterly disillusioned, and distant from God. Friends, church leaders, and Christian organizations had few answers and were at a loss when addressing "divorce for just cause." They seemed determined that I should salvage my marriage.

Psalm 91:14–16 reads, "'Because he loves me,'" says the LORD, "'I will rescue him; I will protect him, for he acknowledges my name. He will call upon me, and I will answer him; I will be with him in trouble,

I will deliver him and honor him. With long life will I satisfy him and show him my salvation.'" It wasn't long before I recognized the truth of this promise, and came to better understand the journey on which God had taken me. Divorce always involves suffering and anguish, but there is joy and abundant grace to be found for all those who bow before Him.

This book has been written for those who have searched and are seeking answers that cannot easily be found. I am delighted to share my own search for God with you, finding the path that best served my family in the midst of unusual circumstances, and the healing that came.

Stick with me and share my journey. I pray that my story will bring light and hope to an issue that affects so many families today—something that has been hidden in the dark recesses of the Christian church for far too long.

Christian media avoids issues that conflict with biblical interpretation on divorce. My writing does not attack religion but supports troubled families seeking help. Experience speaks louder than academic rules, and this book serves as extension when therapeutic marriage counseling falls silent.

PART I
HOPE DENIED

Photo by Michael A. Wollen, www.mindtapmedia.com

CHAPTER 1

MARRIAGE AND THE FAMILY

After a long day at a trade show, I called home from my hotel room in San Antonio, Texas. My oldest son, Perry, answered the phone. After a brief greeting he said that workers had come to the house to put up fences and install a large sundeck in the backyard. This didn't please me because I had instructed my wife Sophie to wait until I got back. I'd planned to make the backyard of our new house into a playground for the children, plant fruit trees, and grow hedges against the street. I was in despair and asked to talk to my wife. After a tense moment that seemed unusually long, Sophie picked up the receiver and said in a low and calm voice, "You'll have to talk to my lawyer," and hung up without saying good-bye. Such abrupt farewells always troubled me.

We had attempted a marriage renewal, and I now realized that the regeneration hadn't worked out as planned. We were back in the same old routine. Building a new family home hadn't improved the marital situation as I had hoped. The cramped space of our previous house had not been the reason for the deteriorating relationship. My wife, driven by her intense mood swings, had fiercely taken off in a dangerous and unpredictable direction. She became assertive and outright destructive, and was doing things on the spur of the moment without considering the consequences.

When I arrived home I noticed that the sundeck occupied a large portion of the backyard. My plan for fruit trees was out the window. I was angry that Sophie used the occasion of my travel to get her own way. She knew that I wanted to do the landscaping myself, but she went ahead, as if to upset me deliberately.

As disappointing as the botched landscaping plan was, the home-coming was even more disheartening. Instead of welcoming me with a smile and a hug, as she had done in the past, Sophie stood at the doorway, arms crossed, unmoved as if made of stone. Walking toward the house, she glared at me as if I were a stranger. Then she spoke up, and in a cold, scornful voice said, "This is my house. You are only allowed in to pack your belongings, and then leave."

I didn't enter the house but headed straight to my office and worked late into the night. This was only one of many episodes that began to unfold at home. All I could do was support my five children to the best of my ability, pretend things were fine, and then wait for an inevitable crisis to happen. It came all too soon.

NERVOUS BREAKDOWN

Another trade show came up in March 1991, this time in Anaheim, California. We decided to turn this occasion into a family holiday and drive. Sophie could visit Disneyland with the children while I attended the conference at the nearby convention center. Everyone thought this was a good idea. My wife needed a holiday, I thought, and this trip would help her unwind. The principal at the school, who was aware of our growing family problems, also agreed and allowed the children to skip their classes.

The first leg of the trip went well and we had fun. Then, all of a sudden, it happened again. I had no idea what triggered Sophie's drastic mood swing. While traveling from San Francisco to Los Angeles, she began yelling at me, saying that I was a miserable father and an unfit husband. She said that I loved other women more than her and that these women would twist me like a rag. She even accused me of being homosexual. That remark hurt me the most, and she knew it.

Sophie may not have realized how much she upset me. Making humiliating remarks in front of the children destroys the respect for a father. *How easy it would be to just miss a curve on that mountain pass in the heavy rain, driving at 70 miles an hour,* I thought. *No one would ever find out, other than blaming the accident on weather conditions.* But this would have been a cowardly move. No calamity is worth risking one's life because the gift of life is too precious. Problems, even if insurmountable at the time, will eventually resolve on God's own timetable.

At the hotel, Sophie was unable to sleep. At 5 o'clock in the morning, she woke me to say she was leaving. She wasn't sure where she was going—either to San Francisco or to our home in Vancouver, Canada. When I couldn't persuade her to stay at the hotel, I recommended that she take a bus to San Francisco and visit her relatives there. We would then pick her up after the conference on our way home. She agreed and I drove her to the bus station.

Sophie seemed unusually agitated. She said detectives were following; that our minivan was fitted with cameras, and that the police were after us. Suddenly, she changed her mind and didn't want to go anymore. We stopped for breakfast and I brought her back to the hotel. She was totally deranged. One moment she clung to me and begged to be loved, the next instant she bit me like a snake.

On our way home we visited Sophie's relatives in San Francisco. It was then when she confessed to me that she had been unfaithful. When she asked me if I had done the same, I assured her that I had never had an intimate relationship with any other woman. I didn't find out whether her confession was true or false. Her mind was too far gone to be rational. My main concern was to get her into a hospital for medical help as quickly as possible.

Driving north on Interstate 5, Sophie's condition grew worse and she had what I believed was a nervous breakdown. She was scared of big trucks and pleaded for me to stop on the wayside and wait for the police to pick us up. She refused to come with us to a restaurant when we stopped for food. "I am not hungry," she protested, and begged to be left alone.

Watching her through the large restaurant window, we saw her sitting in the minivan, motionless, as if in deep thought. Then, all of a sudden, she was gone. After rushing out of the restaurant, we searched the parking lot, the neighboring street, and beyond. She was nowhere to be found. Finally, after increasing the radius of our search to outlying areas, we spotted her in a farmer's field. She was sitting in a fetal position and crying. I gently took her by the hand and guided her back to the car, the children supporting me.

We lodged in Oregon, and Sophie felt better in the morning. After breakfast she wanted to go for a walk in the mountains, but I insisted that we get going. "You are always in a hurry," she protested, and didn't want to budge. As she kept ignoring me and when no amount of urging would make her move, I called the children to help. Her protesting and yelling was much to the embarrassment of the motel guests.

Arriving home that evening, I wanted to take her straight to the hospital, but she refused. I was amazed at how strong she was physically when I tried pushing her into the car seat. As I was unable to manage her, I called her relatives, and when they arrived they realized that she wasn't in her right mind. In some ways, this was a relief to me because my in-laws had always thought I was making things up.

The next morning we had an appointment to sign the ownership papers for our new home. Sophie dressed up in a full-length gold evening gown with an oversized ribbon at the back. I couldn't do much about her choice of clothing, other than to explain to the lawyer that this was a special occasion for her. When the papers were presented to us, she refused to sign. She wouldn't trust anyone. I drove her straight to the hospital. This time she did not resist. At the interview with the doctor, she admitted that she had seen visions and heard voices. The hospital admitted her for treatment.

She was always glad to see me when I visited her in her hospital room, and asked how the children were. She was very kind to me and had the soft and gentle demeanor I so much appreciated in her. I saw the gentle woman again, the one I knew from our courting days. Books and magazines lay on the table beside her bed and she looked well rested. Through the large window, the big city spread out like a huge carpet. The mountains rose majestically to the north, and to the east the mighty Fraser River made its way to the Pacific Ocean, cutting through the landscape like a giant silver band that was gracefully reflecting the evening sun. Inside the room Sophie was protected from a world that was simply too harsh for her.

Will she be able to fulfill her role as a wife and mother again? I wondered. I didn't know what our future held and I fretted that her mental disorder might never get better, perhaps only worse. When I finally said good-bye, Sophie clung to me. "Please don't go," she begged. "Stay a little longer. I miss you." Then she said, "I love you."

During her 15-day stay on a psychiatric ward, life at home was pleasant. I enjoyed the calm and predictable evenings with the children. But all too soon, the psychiatrist called and asked me to pick her up. "Is my wife well?" I inquired. The psychiatrist answered in a tone that sounded strangely ironic, "We have done all we're obligated to do under the circumstances." And then he added, "If the patient refuses treatment, the hospital is relieved of further responsibilities." The official diagnosis was bipolar disorder, also known as manic-depression.

Life after the nervous breakdown was never the same again and the horizon looked darker and stormier than ever. I couldn't do anything right. She kept talking about divorcing me and the amount of support money she wanted. The amount was high. She became scornful and told lies about me to others. She hinted that she wanted to destroy my personal life and ruin the company we had built together.

"Did the mental condition dictate her behavior like a windup toy, or did she act on her own free will?" I asked. "Was she able to reason and have full control of her actions, or was she a slave to her mental condition? Did she believe in her lies, or was she hearing voices, unable to distinguish what was true and what was imagined?" I believed it was a bit of both. She was convinced I was a bad man and wanted me out of her life. No amount of reasoning and explaining could change her mind.

COPING WITH MENTAL ILLNESS

Bipolar disorder, also known as manic-depressive behavior, is a change in the brain that causes severe mood swings. The afflictions can vary from *hypomania*, a mild form of the illness, to full-blown *mania*. People with hypomania are energetic, overflow with ideas, and are charismatic, but are often irritable. Many folks afflicted with the symptoms lead a normal life and hold responsible jobs. They have articulate verbal skills, are socially active, easy to approach, and find pleasure in small things. The person is most productive during the *high,* but this elevated mood cannot be sustained and eventually gives way to depression. The full-blown *mania* is more severe. It affects function, and the person becomes a slave to the affliction. Mania distresses each person differently. Some go into remission and maintain well-controlled mood swings; others suffer from rapid cycles of highs and lows as if bobbing on the ocean in a boat with no power, torn by the waves.

The first sign that something might be wrong with a loved one is a change in everyday routine. The healthy spouse is often the first to notice this transformation. It may begin with a squabble about something trivial. Reasoning no longer works. Nothing satisfies, and trying to calm the aggravation only agitates the situation. An argument breaks out and the healthy spouse wonders what on earth has brought on such a commotion. He or she takes blame for not having handled the situation better. Then, after a few days or weeks, the low turns into exuberant highs of joy and happiness. The affected person explodes with glee and energy, and the previous incident is all but forgotten. As enjoyable as this ecstasy might be, it is short lived. As sunshine gives way to rain, so also will the low mood return, perhaps darker than before.

The symptoms of bipolar manifest themselves in many different ways. During the high the affected person is easy going, likes to talk, is creative, and achieves great things. The mania may be accompanied by a shopping spree and having difficulty sleeping at night. The patient may get overly optimistic and draw up grandiose plans that lack prudence and good judgment. The low cycles are marked with social withdrawal, unusual messiness, sudden loss of interest in favorite activities, pacing for no apparent reason, inability to sit still, prolonged staring with no focus, and deteriorating personal hygiene. The person may make odd remarks while in conversation with others, laugh at something that isn't funny, cry excessively, or not be able to cry. He or she may also display unfounded hostility and anger against certain people, accuse them wrongly, and express a lack of compassion.

In advanced stages, hallucinations can occur. The patient becomes disoriented and sees, hears, and smells things that are not real. This is often associated with delusions and the patient may utter things that are imagined. He or she might assume the role of a prophet, chosen for a spiritual mission, only to fall into helpless depression and wanting to die. Some become overly religious, always talking about God, praying aloud in public, and preaching gloom and doom. At this stage in the illness, a patient must be carefully observed because there is an increased possibility of suicide.

Clinical depression is more than feeling low. Something is wrong medically. The afflicted person knows about the changes and wants to hide the failing mental perception. He or she is embarrassed to talk about the weird and unexplainable phenomenon that is happening in the head. It would be best to seek medical treatment right away but denial is common. The earlier the person can be treated, the better the prognosis will be.

Depression is on the rise in the Western world, and according to studies conducted by the National Alliance for the Mentally Ill (NAMI), about two million U.S. adults suffer from a bipolar disorder. Women are affected twice as often as men. Left untreated, the patient can plunge into absolute hell during the low cycle. There is no fix-all medication, but drugs and therapies help reduce the symptoms.

Mental illness often starts in the late teenage years. In some cases the affliction gets delayed to early adulthood and even later, as was the case with Sophie. I began suspecting that something was wrong when she started telling me strange stories that seemed believable but were untrue. One night she urged me to get out of bed to check an incident that supposedly happened outside the house. Looking around and walking up to the street corner, I found nothing unusual. Coming home from work, she would sometimes say that a truck had followed her, trying to run her over. Concerned about this apparent attempt to hurt her, I attempted to get a better picture by asking for more detail. She had a hard time explaining and told the story again in a more dramatic way. She was unable to deliver pertinent information and could not distinguish between reality and fantasy.

"Would early medical treatment have prevented Sophie's nervous breakdown?" I asked the doctors. The answer was inconclusive, suggesting that each case is different. What the doctors advised, however, was the importance of taking the prescription drugs after a nervous breakdown. Many people go off medication when feeling better, only to suffer a relapse. Each breakdown makes the condition worse.

Sophie suffered several relapses that required hospitalization. She now takes her medication, but this makes her slow and sluggish, a side effect she has to live with. We don't know what brought on her bipolar illness but I suspect genetics. Some of her relatives also suffered from a similar affliction.

PERSONALITY DISORDERS

Many people also suffer from various forms of personality disorders. These are not clinical illnesses but inflict great stress on a marriage nevertheless. A *Harvard Mental Health Letter* (June 2006) describes this condition in a paper titled, "References for Borderline Personality Disorder."

> Personality disorder is defined as stable, pervasive and inflexible patterns of perception, thinking and behavior that cause serious distress or disability. These patterns involve personal relationships, habits of thinking and the control of impulse and emotions. People with personality disorders are difficult to live and work with and respond poorly to stress and change . . . Its typical features are erratic moods, turbulent personal relationships, inability to control anger and destructive behavior. People with borderline personality disorder are often chronically angry and quick to take offense. They become suddenly depressed, irritable, anxious or enraged for reasons not obvious to others. They cannot tolerate solitude or keep company without constant conflict . . . They fear abandonment but repeatedly provoke it by plaguing others with unreasonable demands and complaints.
>
> —Excerpt from *Harvard Mental Health Letter*
> (June 2006)

It is difficult to distinguish between a *personality disorder* and a mild *psychotic illness* because the behavior patterns are similar. There are no defined boundaries and doctors choose medication by trial and error. They insist, however, that a personality disorder and clinical depression are not related and maintain that one does not lead to the other.

I noticed early signs of personality disorder in Sophie soon after our marriage. This was most apparent when traveling together. I didn't think much of it then and thought the symptoms were part of adjusting to married life. Furthermore, Sophie was overly irritable and easily angered before and during premenstrual periods. I knew about this critical time of the month and got prepared. Her joking about the rocky week ahead was easier to take than being smitten unannounced. An estimated eight percent of women suffer from *premenstrual dysphoric*, the official psychiatric term for severe PMS. The disorder is earmarked by irritability, tension, weepiness, and mood swings.

CIRCUMSTANTIAL DEPRESSION

Not all depression is mental illness, nor does feeling low lead to one. Circumstantial depression is normal and occurs if a family pet dies, a loved one gets sick, or one loses a job. Many also feel withdrawn during the dark and cold winter months. It's normal to be down for a short period. Our bodies need revitalizing much like a battery needs recharging. We must come out of this melancholy and feel happy again.

We all experience mood swings. Those with pronounced lows and highs are often the more engaging and creative folks than the level-headed counterparts. We know of many famous artists and masterminds who are, or have been, affected by severe mood swings. Ludwig Van Beethoven; Abraham Lincoln; Diana, Princess of Wales; Harrison Ford; and Ben Stiller are just a few names that come to mind. These talented people have accomplished astonishing things during their highs and have gained deep insights when down and out. Feeling overjoyed for a few days and then going into a low as a counterbalance is no cause for concern. Just as the high and low barometric pressure brings sunshine and rain, so also should we harness these mood swings for creative purposes to enrich lives and bring joy to others.

We seek to do better with each passing generation and look forward to a rewarding life, but God has His own plan. Virtuous living is no guarantee for a successful marriage. Obstacles placed in the way may interfere with our noble desires.

CHAPTER 2

GROWING UP WITH DIVINE HOPES

A LOOK BACK

I grew up in a conservative farming community in rural Switzerland. Everybody knew one another and we went to church on Sundays. My three brothers and I were altar boys, as was my father. We were proud to serve the church because this assured us a special place in heaven, or so we were told. My mother said that praying 4,000 Hail Marys during Advent would grant a special wish, but that many prayers was a large number for a small schoolboy. I had to recite an average of 130 Hail Marys every day and used a school abacus to keep track. I can't remember exactly what I wished, other than wanting better school grades and when grown up, being married to a good wife, having a nice family, and enjoying a successful career.

The parish priest held the ultimate power in our village and didn't like interference; the teachers were one level below him. Together they reigned with supreme authority, and we obeyed all the rules. Woe if we messed up! The parish priest and the teachers would dive in and get the full support from the parents. We kids were always outnumbered.

Given this conservative background, we were shielded from modern temptations such as stealing, pornography, and drug abuse. We couldn't understand why people would smoke and drink if these were harmful to the body. We almost had to die before Mother would give us a headache pill because such medicine was believed to be bad for our health. Once a month we went to confession, going through the Ten Commandments and faithfully enumerating our sins. We made sure that our sin-account was accurate—not too high, or the penance would be severe, and not too low because we knew someone higher up was keeping score. The old nuns from our convent also went to regular confession, and we boys wondered what sins they could have committed. They were so saintly.

Mother reminded us to honor and respect the girls. She referred to them as "Holy Mary," the mother of Jesus. I always thought that the girls were smarter than us boys because they could talk fast, read well, and spot any spelling mistake. They were always right and we boys could never win an argument with them. This was fine with us and we accepted it as a way of life. The girls wore colorful dresses and stayed inside the house while we boys worked in the fields and got dirty. I looked at them as flowers, beautiful and pure. We boys were more like the bark of an apple tree—rough and rowdy.

I had an accordion and played to visitors at home, at carnivals, and at village parades. As enjoyable as this was, I was fascinated with playing the piano. One day I mentioned to my schoolteacher, who was also the church organist, that I would like to learn to play the piano. He looked at me dejectedly and, trying to discourage me, said, "Look, you are a farm boy, and it would be better if you played the horn. Then you can join the village brass band." My father and oldest brother played in the village band, but this was not for me.

Several times a year we joined in prayer processions, walking to neighboring villages to attend Mass. How we altar boys disliked doing this! Imagine walking by a cheese-dairy, the very place where we boys delivered milk on a dog-pulled cart after school in ragged street clothes, now parading in our heavenly church attire, praying the rosary, and carrying the crucifix high on a flagpole! I blushed and turned my head when I recognized familiar faces.

One afternoon I went to church all by myself to pray. I was in grade four and wanted to remind God of my long wish list. Then an embarrassing thing happened. As I knelt alone in the pew in the quiet church, the side door slowly opened and the parish priest entered. He was a holy man of great stature whom everyone in the village respected and feared. As if caught in a forbidden act, I tried to escape, but the priest came closer, smiled, and exchanged kind words with me. Later he suggested to my parents that I should become a priest. I struggled with this thought for a while but then decided not to follow this path. After this episode, I stopped going to the church alone, lest I get caught again.

I have many fond memories of growing up on a farm. I enjoyed the family outings to visit relatives and acquaintances by horse and wagon on faraway farms. Mother and Dad would sit up high on the front seat of the open wagon and we boys would huddle on the two wooden benches at the back. Fritz, the horse, was the engine. In the winter we would switch to a horse-drawn sleigh. Dad would fasten the jingle bells and Mother would bundle us up really well to keep warm, because the winters were cold. Galloping through the snow-covered winter wonderland with the sound of jingle bells was an unforgettable experience. All too soon, cars filled the roads and such outings became history.

The winters were very cold, and I remember minus-40–degree Celsius temperatures. The Holy water in our bedrooms would freeze, a thick layer of ice would form on the kitchen windows, and during the 30-minute walk to school and church, our pants and scarf would become frozen stiff. Sometimes the snow would get so deep that we had to go by ski. We all made it through these long winters and were seldom late. Some children had to walk far greater distances than us, and there was no school bus. Springtime came as a welcomed relief.

Farm life was tough and the daily grind left us boys with little free time to pursue our hobbies. Dad wanted to instill in us the same dedication to farming as his father had passed on to him, but we boys had different ambitions. I was interested in electronics and enjoyed fixing old radios. I didn't mind helping out during the busy seasons, but the relentless farm toil soon became a drag. To escape, we gravitated toward the women's quarter in the house. Unfortunately, Mother also had many chores from which we couldn't escape.

I remember the occasional beating I got from my dad. Physical punishment produced a profound guilt feeling as a small boy, fearing that I had done something terribly wrong. As I grew older, this type of retribution shifted to resentment, and a rift formed between Dad and me. I felt I wasn't measuring up and became insecure. All I wanted was someone to put an arm around me and say, "You'll be all right, lad, you'll make it." Such affection was uncommon in Old Europe and almost nonexistent in my family. Although my parents never gave us praise, they expressed their affection in different ways. Nevertheless, I felt fenced in and thought of an escape. I wanted to follow my older brother, Joe, in emigrating to the big land of America.

After completing my four-year postgraduate education, the emigration papers arrived all too quickly, and in the summer of 1966, I bought a one-way plane ticket to Vancouver, Canada. I packed a small suitcase and withdrew the equivalent of 100 dollars as seed money to kick-start my new life.

On the day of my departure, Mother reminded me to go over to the barn and say good-bye to my father. I would have forgotten had she not told me because our relationship had become distant and cold. I didn't know how Dad felt about my leaving. I never discussed my plans with him, nor did he inquire about my ambitions in life.

My father looked worried when I walked into the cow barn. He knew I'd come to say good-bye. He struggled to keep his emotions and his eyes were watery. I had never seen him this way before. He was always strong and in command. He tried to smile but had a hard time sustaining it. The worry lines on his forehead made him look older than his age. We both knew there was much unfinished business— those important father-and-son conversations that never took place. I didn't want to bring them up now, nor did he. My focus was to get to the airport in time to catch my plane. My mind was already miles away. I was excited, and perhaps a bit apprehensive about going. After all, it was my first flight in an airplane, and it was a one-way trip to an unknown land. This wasn't the time to get sentimental. Dad's handshake was warm and cordial. I hopped into the neighbor's car waiting at the house, and off we went to the Zurich airport, my mother accompanying me.

Before walking to the departure gate at the airport, I noticed tears flowing down my mother's cheeks. I had never seen her cry before. She was a tough woman who kept her emotions under control. Perhaps she was thinking of my brother Joe, who had left for Canada one year before. I wasn't going to become emotional now, and besides, I had to run. Walking toward the plane on the tarmac I glanced back at the terminal building one last time as if to say farewell to Switzerland. The umbilical cord had been cut and I was on my way to a new and unfamiliar world.

I wanted to prove to my father that I could make it on my own and was eager to try anything. I knew my limitations but these, I thought, would melt away in the new country.

All too soon I realized that starting a new life was more difficult than I had anticipated. My English was poor, good jobs were hard to find, and the pay was low. I took on jobs that I would never have considered in my old country. I was often laid off, leaving me in a desperate search for a new job to pay for food and rent. I was too proud to go home to my parents as the prodigal son did in the Bible. Deep in my heart I knew I would eventually make it.

A son might try plowing his own way, but he does better with the blessing of his father. The furrow the father carves for the son's footsteps serves as a sure channel in which to walk in unfamiliar territory when building identity in a young life. Taking the map and compass from the father's hands provides solid guidance—trying to draw one's own, as I did, leads to many twists and turns before finding the path that fits the plan. Blessed is the son whose father prepares a path.

FINDING A GIRL

I was now comfortably settled in the new country and had a steady job, but I got lonely living by myself in a rented basement suite. I was on the lookout for companionship, a nice girl to spend my life together in marriage. This, as it turned out, didn't come easily.

Several years had passed when I noticed four girls singing at the church I attended. The four-part harmony reverberated beautifully against the wooden church ceiling as they sang. The guitar accompaniment was simple but well rehearsed and precise. Above all, the girls were good looking and merited a closer look. So I decided to wait after the service. And as they walked by, I introduce myself as a recording technician.

"You sing well," I complimented, and then asked, "Would you like to come to my recording studio to tape a few songs?" Excited about this opportunity, they agreed.

My studio was nothing more than a Sony reel-to-reel tape recorder with two studio-grade microphones I had set up in my sparsely furnished living room. I had done many recordings with a folk group in that room before, and one made it to a 45 rpm single that was sold at a folk festival in Ontario. Perhaps it was the low ceiling and the wooden paneling that brought out the quality of the human voice and the richness of the acoustical guitar.

I had already set up the mics and queued the tape recorder when the girls arrived in the afternoon. I heard their giggles before they knocked on the door. All four were in their early 20s. They had come from the Philippines and were sharing an apartment.

After a few warm-up songs, I asked each girl to perform solo. Hesitant at first, they soon showed their talents and performed well. One girl caught my special attention. She possessed natural beauty, was well mannered and radiated with a calm and engaging charisma. When she smiled, a set of perfect teeth like pearls sparkled from her red lips. I couldn't take my eyes off her and I observed every move she made. Her name was Sophie, and I later learned that she had won a beauty-pageant in the Philippines. She had earned a university degree and held a well-paid accounting position at Simon Fraser University. Her father was a lawyer and businessman, and she had many brothers and sisters.

After the recording session I asked Sophie for her phone number, and she was kind enough to give it to me. The next day I phoned her, ostensibly thanking her and the other girls for coming to my studio. After a few more phone calls, we developed a casual friendship and we began liking each other. The long and warm summer evening provided the perfect setting for long walks. We talked about everything and shared the same views on many things. My heart soared: Could she be the one for me?

But this hope was soon crushed. It was during a singing rehearsal at their apartment when Sophie confessed to me that she was engaged to marry a physician in New York. Her friends knew about this all along but didn't want to spoil the romance. Now, everyone was in tears and I had a hard time keeping my composure. My voice was choking because I knew this was the end of a beautiful friendship—a relationship that simply was too good to be true. The girls then told me that Sophie's fiancé had given her an expensive diamond ring before moving to Vancouver. Not wanting to break up their relationship, I quietly left the party and kept my distance.

By chance we met again. Sophie was delighted to see me, and from the ensuing conversation I gleaned that she wanted to keep in touch. This was both a surprise and a thrill to me. I knew, of course, that she was engaged. Another man had promised to marry her and the ring was the symbol of this covenant. "Material possessions are not important to me," Sophie assured me, and kept the ring out of my sight.

Sophie had a traumatic upbringing. When she was a teenager, her father left the family of ten children to marry a younger woman. Soon afterward, a flood damaged their stately family home in the outskirts of Manila. The family was not able to afford the repairs and meet the mortgage payments, and the bank foreclosed on the house. To help her cash-strapped mother, Sophie sent money to the Philippines. She lived very frugally and only purchased items she absolutely needed.

We went on seeing each other and our relationship grew stronger. The longer we dated, the more she seemed to distance herself from her fiancé. She acted as if he didn't exist and she was drawn closer to me with every passing week. I began hinting about marriage and she had no problem with this. Then finally, I proposed, and to my delight she accepted.

Sophie still needed to break the relationship with her fiancé. When hearing about the changed marriage plan, he jumped on a plane and flew to Vancouver. Sophie was apprehensive about meeting him, not knowing what to expect. The visit was cordial and he accepted the change without visible heartbreak. The engagement was dissolved and Sophie was allowed to keep her ring. We then decided to become engaged ourselves, and set our wedding date for October 1971.

As part of the marriage preparations, the church mandated that we attend marriage preparation courses. Listening to the many possible marital problems suggested at these group meetings, we shrugged our shoulders and said, "Surely, these difficulties are directed at other couples and not at us." We loved each other and thought that anyone could resolve these differences by simply talking them over. After all, we had a lifetime to do this.

GETTING MARRIED

Nervously, I sat in the front pew of the very church where we'd first met. A large congregation had assembled behind me and we were patiently awaiting the arrival of the bride. But none came! An awkward silence arose. The wait seemed strangely long and I got uneasy. It must have been 30 minutes or perhaps an hour that we waited. Something was wrong and I couldn't figure out why Sophie had not arrived. Then, at last, I heard voices. The church door opened and the bride entered with her party.

My heart triumphed as I saw my wife-to-be walking down the aisle, gracefully moving, step-by-step, as if floating on air. She wore the most beautiful wedding gown imaginable and her face was filled with radiant joy. She smiled and her sparkling teeth made her countenance shine like the golden sun in the early morning hours. Closer and closer she came, until she finally stood beside me. Hand in hand we walked up to the wedding pew that had been prepared for us, and together we knelt in front of the altar.

A vocal group played "Love's Yearning," a song I had written. The music sounded beautiful in the church with its tall wooden ceiling. The melody flowed freely and seemed never-ending. The words conveyed a message of yearning for love and happiness. I couldn't help but thank God for having answered my lifelong prayers. I felt as if the heavens above had opened and the angels were partaking in our jubilation.

A beautiful wedding deserves an equally delightful honeymoon, and ours was planned to be just that. I had reserved a room at Harrison Hot Springs Hotel, a short drive from Vancouver. I envisioned a honeymoon room overlooking the majestic mountains and the beautiful lake that made the hotel so famous. But this was not going to happen. Arriving at the check-in counter, the receptionist said in a stern voice, "I am sorry, the hotel is fully booked."

"This must be a mistake," I replied. "I made reservations many weeks in advance."

"Sir, your room has been given away because of your *late arrival*," he said in a firm voice.

I argued that it was only seven o'clock in the evening; and besides, this was our *honeymoon*. The clerk didn't budge. The answer was simple and clear: There was no room in the inn.

Not wanting to disappoint my new wife, I suggested we go to the hotel's dining room and enjoy a nice dinner. This would give us time to draw up a new plan for our first night together. When we arrived at the restaurant, the waiter looked at us as if we were escaped convicts and said in a derisive voice, "Sorry, I can't let you in."

"Why not?" I demanded.

"You're not wearing proper apparel," he said, meaning I wasn't wearing a tie and Sophie was in shorts.

Not wanting to argue further, we left the hotel and strolled down to the lake. We found a hamburger stand and, not being familiar with the area, ordered two hamburgers and ate them at the lakeside. Searching for a room, we later checked into a motel on a busy highway. It just so happened that this very night a rowdy dance party had gathered on the upstairs floor. Our bedroom couldn't have been in a worse location. We were directly below the dance floor! There was loud music and thump, thump, thump all night long.

Was this honeymoon a sign of what was to come? At first I thought it was sheer bad luck, but as we entered a difficult marriage together, I realized that God had given us a foretaste of what was to come. Was it a coincidence that the bridal party had a flat tire on the way to church that morning, delaying the wedding ceremony? Was it customary for a hotel to give away a reserved honeymoon room when the rightful party arrived during daylight? Was it common for a waiter to refuse entry to a dining room for guests in casual attire? And why was our room located directly under a dance floor? Our Good Lord sends His teasers with a touch of humor.

MARRIED LIFE

The first years of married life were enjoyable. Our love life was good and Sophie wanted to do the love act at the most awkward places, as if to assign secret "marks of love" on this earth that only the two of us would know.

Like any new husband, I needed to get housebroken and soon realized that being married was different from growing up with my three brothers on the farm. By nature, Sophie was very jealous and didn't allow me to look at another women. More than that, I needed to learn how to satisfy my better half when she was down. Feeling low and insecure, she would fall into my arms and beg, "Do you still love me?" "Yes, I still love you," I would assure her. With time, I repeated this promise so many times that I began sounding like a broken record.

Sophie began telling me about her frightening nightmares, and they began to worry her. She would see me riding away on a white horse and disappear in the dusk, never to come back again. I couldn't imagine any man doing such a cruel thing, and I would promise that I would always stay with her.

Her mood swings began worrying me. There were times when she was exceedingly happy and everything was wonderful. Then, for unknown reasons, communication would abruptly stop. She would ignore me, become cold and distant, and not say a word to me for days. When I asked what I had done wrong, she would always find something she didn't like. I was at a loss for what to do and felt guilty, thinking I had caused her sadness. And then, out of the blue, she would fly into my arms again, hold me tight, and ask if I still loved her.

Were these mood swings and insecurities an early sign of clinical depression, the onslaught of mental illness? I thought that her anxiety attacks and mood swings might be connected with her childhood upbringing and the worry she had experienced when her father left the family. She told me of threats her dad had made that caused the children to fear for their lives. This was at a young and delicate age, and the memories were still fresh in her mind. All I could do was to assure her that she was in safe hands and that I would always love her.

MEETING MY PARENTS

In 1973 we made the long-anticipated pilgrimage to Switzerland. I wanted to introduce my new bride to my parents. This was to be a highlight of my life, a voyage no longer made solo but in company of my dear wife. *Being married would give me new status*, I thought, *and override the difficulties I had experienced growing up on the farm.*

We first visited England and then took an overnight train, arriving in Lucerne in the early morning hours. My younger brother picked us up at the train station. As we drew closer to the village where I grew up, my heart began pounding with apprehension. I wondered how my parents were and how Sophie would be received. As we neared the farm, everything looked so much smaller than I remembered. The fields on which we worked as boys had shrunk, and even the stately farmhouse had lost its stature and looked small.

My mother and my father waved as we drove in. Looking at them closer, I thought they had aged a little. I introduced my wife and she was welcomed with a warm handshake and a smile. Smiling and nodding was all we could do because my parents didn't speak English and Sophie's acquired German was not sufficient to strike up a conversation. I am certain that my mom and dad would have enjoyed conversing, but I had to translate the compliments offered to Sophie. Whenever we had language difficulties, my mother would always bring up the biblical story of the Tower of Babel (Gen. 11), in which different civilizations experienced language barriers and could no longer converse with each other. The Bible says that the project of building the large tower eventually failed.

The first few days at my parents' farm were cordial and friendly. And then, it happened. My mother was weeding in the strawberry field when she stood up, looked at me crossly, and asked, "Did you *have* to marry Sophie?"

Surprised about this question, I mumbled, "No. Why do you ask? She was my choice."

An awkward silence fell between us. My mother bent down and continued her work, weeding more intensely than before. Her comment troubled me. It suggested that she didn't approve of my choice of a wife. I didn't want to discuss the issue further and left the field. I knew that my first obligation was toward Sophie and not my mother. As I walked up the hill toward the house, the question began burning in my heart, "Did I make a mistake in marrying Sophie? Does her being

Asian cause a rift in our family genealogy? Is my mother discriminating against a different culture?"

Flashbacks of my upbringing projected before my eyes, reminding me of why I had left my home in the first place. I was a dreamer, an individual who thought "outside the box." I wanted to be set free, unhindered from strict parental control. More than anything, I begged to be accepted and respected for who I was.

I didn't tell Sophie about my mother's comment, but Sophie could feel the rift. An eerie estrangement formed between the two women. The language barrier and the different cultures made this worse. Farm life is harsh for city people as it is, but most troubling of all, Sophie felt rejected as a member of my family. She was looked upon as a foreigner. This was during the time when the so-called "boat people" arrived from Asia and flooded Europe. People kept asking if she were one of them. My mother was not amused.

Mother liked to have me around in the kitchen to chat. Sophie would join us for a while, but not being able to understand the language upset her. She would withdraw into the bedroom and sulk. When I tried cheering her up, she would give me the cold shoulder and brush me off. I had never seen her this way, and the rejection began worrying me.

"The first thing I'll do when I get home is divorce you," she hissed. Such words did not go over well with me. Even visiting my friends was a downer. The conversation over tea and cookies resembled a funeral assembly more than a happy reunion. Nobody spoke English, and Sophie found my friends boring and uninteresting. It was as if a dark cloud had formed over our relationship. It was a wedge that divided us into two worlds and two cultures.

At last, the long visit drew to a close and we said good-bye to my folks. We were looking forward to going home and living our own lives again. Sophie's mood changed the moment we left the farm. She was outright jubilant when we boarded the train to Zurich. We were on our own again, united as a couple. Immediately she clung to me as if she hadn't seen me in months and expressed how difficult the stay had been, especially around my mother. We visited our friend in Zurich who spoke English, and Sophie was able to converse freely again.

CHAPTER 3

EMERGING MENTAL PROBLEMS

STARTING A FAMILY

How nice it was to be home again, living in our little home we had purchased earlier. This post-Word War II house was very small and had only one bedroom. The front door opened into the living room and the back door into the kitchen. A gas stove in the living room heated the entire home. I moved the hot water tank to the attic to gain extra space, and hooked up the dryer in the storage area to make room for the refrigerator in the kitchen.

We had bought the house with the plan to make it larger. Two years later, with building permit in hand, the house-lifters arrived early one morning and raised the little house high into the air. Within a few months the dwelling took on a new dimension, growing into a stately home three times the original size. Remodeling my own home gave me immeasurable satisfaction.

During the construction our daughter Holly was born. With a newborn, life changed and Sophie devoted most of her time to the baby. She enjoyed feeding her and helping with her first steps. *How beautiful it was when Sophie sang to her, I thought. My wife's sweet voice was heavenly and life couldn't get any better. There is nothing more uplifting than a mother singing to a child. These memories are unforgettable.* Later, we were blessed with four more children—all boys—and we enjoyed each one to the fullest.

After two years of dedicated weekend work, I finally managed to finish the house and invited my parents for a visit. I felt good showing off my accomplishment, and indeed, Mother and Dad were most surprised to see this white two-story house with the fancy woodwork in the living room, hallways, and kitchen. *Dad must be proud of me,* I thought, but he never said so. Later, my mother wrote that Dad couldn't stop talking about the house I had built. I am certain that he wanted to say something, but he simply couldn't.

Sadly, shortly after the visit Dad suffered a stroke and never fully recovered. His speech was labored and we could no longer engage in meaningful conversations. Any discussions with the slightest negative hint of the past caused his eyes to well up with tears. He later died of complications.

How I wished we could have discussed the unfinished business between us while there still was time, I thought, when I saw Dad lying in his casket. The unspoken words went to the grave, silenced forever. God gives us many opportunities to mend the past but we often neglect to use the allotted time wisely.

THE ENGAGEMENT RING

We had now been married for seven years, and life was good. Our marriage was stable and I laid my earlier concerns about her mood swings to rest. They were controllable. I was promoted to a manager's position at General Electric, and our combined incomes with both of us working allowed for a comfortable living.

During this gratifying time Sophie retrieved the engagement ring that had been given to her by the former fiancé. Until now, the ring had been stowed away in a safe-deposit box at the bank. I would have preferred that she sold the ring, but Sophie began negotiating a remount and adding a very precious diamond. She never disclosed the price of the upgrade to me other than to say it was expensive and that the investment would be worth the price.

The remounted ring was truly a masterpiece. It featured a large protruding diamond in the middle, flanked by smaller stones around as if to adorn the master. Although it was strikingly beautiful, I was uneasy when Sophie wore it in my presence. Even though redone and made new, it was still a gift from another man. Why did she want to wear it when we were happily married and had our own family, I asked?

Sophie felt that both of us should enjoy the fruit of our labors and she wanted me to buy something nice too. I had been playing classical music on an old upright piano, but my dream had been to own a grand piano. After much hesitation, a beautiful Yamaha C3 finally arrived at our new home. This instrument added a powerful presence in our living room.

Little did I know that this time characterized the climax of our married life. Something worrisome began to emerge—it was the beginning of lavish spending. We had always been very careful with money and I couldn't understand why Sophie would suddenly change. The ring wasn't the only item acquired. She purchased the *Encyclopedia Britannica* even though we already had a 22-volume set by a different publisher. Then she bought expensive ceramic figurines and fancy fur coats. We had agreed to discuss all major purchases beforehand, but this agreement no longer applied.

Purchases made her happy, but the momentary ecstasy would soon wear off and she would lose interest in the acquired possessions. When the kids smashed the expensive ceramic figurines playing ball in the living room, she didn't seem to get upset. Even though I didn't like this clutter, I was more heartbroken than her, seeing the broken pieces on the floor.

The presence of the ring began having a strange effect. It meant trouble. Wearing it signaled a rough ride ahead. It became a weather barometer of sorts, foretelling the mood for the week. My predictions were mostly correct and I could prepare myself for a bumpy ride. When the storm passed and the sunshine returned, Sophie would stow the ring away again. We would enjoy several weeks or months of good times before the dark clouds would form again. This uncertain time would coincide with the reappearance of the ring. As time went on, the ring began playing a larger part in our marriage and living with Sophie became difficult.

STRUGGLING MARRIAGE

The following chapters describe the tension and devastation an advancing psychiatric disorder can bring to a marriage and the family. It is prudent that I only mention a few episodes, but those illustrated will give plenty of evidence to the suffering inflicted on the spouse and children. In no way do I want to harm, discredit, defame, dishonor, or blame anyone. I simply want to make the reader aware of abnormal behavior (should that pattern be visible in your loved ones) so you can assist and get early help.

Some folks may think that the episodes I demonstrate are exaggerated and dramatized. They are not. Many spouses suffer quietly under a repressive yoke of living with an unreasonable partner. The faithful spouse may not speak up and seek help, but selflessly accepts the burden, doing what is right for the family, praying for a miracle to happen, and hoping for better times to come. By sharing my stories I am sending a message to hurting spouses and offer compassion to say that you are not alone. The suffering is mutual.

Sophie's condition worsened with the birth of each child, especially from the third one on. She loved children and wanted more. During her pregnancies, she blossomed and life with her was easy. This made me think that she might have a hormonal imbalance and I suggested that she see a doctor. The notion of her having an estrogen deficiency did not go over well and the subject was dropped once and for all.

Sophie became disorganized and her illogical habits began to annoy me. The house turned into a huge mess and the laundry piled halfway up to the ceiling. She preferred buying new stuff at the mall because shopping gave her a boost and a sense of satisfaction. Housecleaning, if any, only started minutes before leaving for church or other outings.

Her cooking became erratic. There was either no food or too much, creating leftovers for days. So we agreed that I would do the cooking and she would clean the dishes. One Sunday evening, after I had prepared a big family meal of hash browns and meat, I called everyone to the table. Sophie sauntered over to the stove, lifted the lid, and said, "Yuck!" Turning to the children, she shouted, "Who wants to go to a restaurant?" Naturally they wanted to go, and off they went, leaving me alone at home to nibble on a meal made for six. When Sophie and the kids came back, stuffed and cheerful, I was unable to explain to her that this episode was upsetting to me. She saw nothing wrong and did it again at other times, leaving me to eat the food I had cooked by myself.

Then Sophie ordered a large custom-made aquarium and put it in our already cramped dinette. Soon, she added cages filled with birds and gerbils. Our house became a zoo. She then insisted on getting a ping-pong table for our living room, which I denied because of space. Next, she wanted an aluminum canopy at the back of our house. I advised her against it, saying that such a roof overhang would make the kitchen and dinette dark. She agreed, but when I came home from work one evening, the workers had already started with the installation. They ripped off the custom-fitted gutters that provided a beam-like façade for the balcony above. I had spent all summer installing those gutters. They extended the entire width of the house and I was quite proud of my handiwork. Sophie then admitted that the new canopy wasn't right and had it removed.

I never installed the gutters again. For a long time the debris lay in the yard, overgrown with grass, before I finally cut up the wood for the fireplace. Refitting the pieces with the many angles would have been too time consuming, and I was not in the mood to rebuild something that had been destroyed against my will.

I bring up this episode because this marked the end of an era. Until that time, I had enjoyed doing home improvements. It was my hobby. But now my spirit was broken and I felt the efforts I'd made had been taken in vain.

Despite the dark moments, the heavy clouds would lift from time to time and the sun would break through again. Our hearts would lighten and we would enjoy a few weeks of blissful happiness. These were some of the finest moments in our marriage and made up for the less desirable seasons. They brought new hope into our hearts, giving us optimism that the worst might be over, and sunnier days lay ahead. Sophie would embrace me tenderly, admit her failures, and ask for forgiveness. With her hot tears burning against my face, she would confess that she hadn't always been the best wife and promised to do better. No one could do this better than her. Her loving kindness formed an incredible closeness between us during such affectionate moments. Likewise, I'd promise to try harder to avoid arguments. We would pray together, asking God to heal our marriage and to bring lasting happiness.

As much as we enjoyed these precious moments and wanted to keep them alive, these phantoms were only an oasis in a dry desert. As time went on, our marriage became increasingly more difficult, and I got lost in the arid and inhospitable wilderness, not knowing which way to turn.

REGRET

I was aware that other families were also struggling and had problems with their marriages, but ours was different in that I was unable to reason with Sophie. I knew little about psychiatric disorders and pleaded with her to see a doctor. Instead of admitting the encroaching illness, she blamed the worsening family situation on me. We argued a lot and our disputes got so tense that I often walked away, frustrated and exhausted. This only infuriated her more.

Sunday mornings were the most dreaded times of the week. Getting the kids ready for church is a challenging undertaking for any family. We had to find twenty socks and shoes that somehow matched. Once dressed, we put each kid into the car, and by the time the last one was loaded, the first ones had sprung loose again and needed to be found. In church the kids were noisy and disruptive. They pulled silly pranks and I had to take them outside most of the time.

It was around Easter when I bought Sophie a bouquet of carnations. I wanted her to experience the delicate fragrance of these fine flowers, memories that reminded me of springtime on the farm. To my shock and horror, I found the carnations in the garbage the very next morning. Not wanting to go to waste I retrieved them, took them to the office, and placed them in the reception area where our secretary worked. As she often did, Sophie stopped by the office on her way home that day.

While working on my project at home in the evening, the workshop door suddenly tore open and Sophie burst in, clutching the flowers in her hands. With rapid movements she tore the long-stemmed carnations into shreds and threw them at my feet. Then she tossed an old sleeping bag at me and locked the door. Before I knew it, she was gone.

What on earth happened? I thought. *What have I done wrong now?* I had never seen her so angry.

It was getting late and I wanted to go to bed. Grabbing the door handle I noticed that I was indeed locked out. Installing bolts that locked on both sides of a door posed a major pitfall and did more than keeping the children out of my workshop—they kept me from getting in. I knocked and yelled for someone to open the door, but the house stayed quiet. There was no stirring from within. I went back to work, but soon got too tired to continue. When my repeated shouts went unanswered, I searched for an alternative entry. Stepping outside, I noticed that the kitchen window was ajar and was able to crawl in. In bed, Sophie turned away from me and articulated how much she hated me. She gave no reason for the anger, and no dialogue was possible.

I was at a loss for what to do. Sophie appeared normal to outsiders, was articulate and believable in her persuasive manners. The in-laws supported her fully and didn't see anything wrong. When I expressed my concerns in seeking assistance, they criticized me and said that I was making things up. Misunderstandings arose and our cordial friendship began to wane. I became the villain who had nothing good to say about Sophie, and I was seen as the source of our growing family problems. I was outnumbered, my explanations held little weight, and my popularity hit rock bottom.

Stressed out, I called my church one Sunday afternoon and said that I was deeply troubled and needed help. "Sorry, I am unable to assist," said the man at the rectory in a cold voice, and hung up. Being ignored at this critical moment was very disappointing, because we had supported this church for many years and all our children had been baptized there.

I then called my former family doctor, who had been my landlord at one time. I knew him well and I looked up to him as to a father. Of course, I knew that he couldn't solve the psychiatric problem of my wife over the phone, but I just needed someone to talk to. He listened for a while and then said with a gasping voice, "You have a difficult time on your hands."

There comes a time when a burden gets so heavy that one needs to unload. We are prepared to talk to anyone, even a stranger, and tell our story. We want to be heard and understood; we want compassion in our agony. For many, opening up and discussing the crisis releases stress. Marriage is meant to share such burden, but when the relationship is falling apart, this becomes unworkable. Lucky is the partner who finds compassion with the spouse.

Sophie had been such a caring spouse. She knew how to lift me up when I was down. She was able to carry my burden in a selfless way when I needed help. Oh, how good it felt to hear her encouraging words. How easy it was to share my inner feelings and bear the load together. There is nothing more rewarding than being able to carry the troubles within the bounds of marriage. This gentle nature was now gone, and instead of giving support, she turned against me in a ghastly manner.

I finally decided to phone my close friend and reveal my problems. Frank and Mary had married one year before us and had three children by now. I first talked to Frank, and when he realized that this was a personal matter, he passed the receiver to Mary. He said that his wife was more experienced in such personal matters, and she was.

Airing marriage problems to a third party causes a serious psychological rift between a husband and wife. By opening the floodgate and sharing my troubles with someone else, I turned against Sophie without knowing and built an invisible wall between us. I became a traitor who released information that should have been kept personal and confidential within the confines of marriage. Exposing the innermost secrets made me two-faced; I was trying to find sympathy from my friends. Sophie and I were no longer one, but divided individuals. I was a refuge adrift in the ocean, seeking help from the outside.

Although outwardly wrong, sharing problems with close associates helps relieve pain. I knew that Frank and Mary would keep this a secret, and they did. From that time on, whenever my heart was heavy, Mary would call me at the office and ask how things were going. She was a wise woman and just listened. At the end of our talk she would ask if we could pray, to which I readily agreed. This lifted me up and I was able to carry on. Finally I asked her one day how she knew that I was having a particularly hard time that day. "The Lord told me," she said confidently.

Astonished about this reply, it began dawning on me that the Lord sends ordinary people when church and secular organizations fail.

I realized that our home situation had gone from bad to worse when Sophie began hinting that I should move out. Reading the newspaper, she would politely say, "They have nice apartments in New Westminster. Why don't you move into one of them? The kids can always visit you." I was dead set against moving out because of the children.

And then a most disturbing incident happened. Going to bed one evening, Sophie yanked my shoulder and in fierce anger yelled, "I hate you. Our relationship is over." Raging with fury, she blamed me for everything that was going wrong.

"I never loved you," she yelled. "My affections toward you were all faked." Her eyes burned with fire as if a demonic spirit possessed her. Her face was red like flames. Her breathing was heavy and her chest swelled and ebbed with deep emotion.

Eventually she calmed down, and from that time on it was as if her brain had been rewired. She started acting like a teenager and said that she had to discover herself. Together with two men in their twenties, she organized a rock band and stayed away until late at night, ostensibly practicing.

Sophie then hired a landscaper and had all shrubbery removed that so nicely decorated the front garden of our house. On her orders, the contractor filled the brick-encased flowerbeds with low-grade dirt. I could hardly believe my eyes when I came home that evening. A once lush garden that I enjoyed maintaining had turned into a wasteland! "The shrubs had grown too large," Sophie uttered without emotion when I ask her why she had done this audacity.

I tried to salvage my prize rhododendron but it was too badly mangled. It had rich foliage all year around. Every spring, while it was in full bloom, I took pictures with the children standing in front. These photos delighted my mother in Switzerland. Now the once-thriving bush lay dying in the driveway. I also grieved over the lilac tree at the side of the house that she had cut down. Every spring, the flowers from this mature tree filled our property with an unforgettable fragrance, reminding us of God's power in conquering the cold of winter and bringing new life in spring.

During this trying time, I received a letter in the mail, marked "Personal and Confidential." It didn't take me long to discover what it was all about; the plain envelope pointed at legal matters. Opening it, I found a divorce petition prepared by Sophie's lawyer. I put it aside and didn't sign.

Sophie then decided to move to her own apartment. For once I didn't have to help. The in-laws came and loaded her belongings into a van. During the move I took the children to a park, but their mood was somber; they knew what was happening. Pointing to unusual flowers and watching the animals play did little to lift their spirits.

Sophie's departure hit us hard but we managed surprisingly well on our own. This gave me a preview of how it would be to manage the family by myself. I soon began enjoying the relaxed and predictable evenings. Meanwhile, Sophie began missing the children and started to drop in after work. She ate with us and then asked me to drop her off at her apartment because she didn't drive. Then something unexpected happened. After 19 years of service as an accountant, Sophie was let go from her work at Simon Fraser University.

No longer earning an income, Sophie asked me if she could move back home and live with us again. Without hesitation, I agreed and took her back. By opening the door I wanted to demonstrate that I still had hope for our marriage. We renewed our marriage vows, forgave each other, and attended a Marriage Encounter Weekend for the second time. Marriage Encounter Weekend is a three-day weekend seminar that teaches couples to strengthen their marriages.

I recognized that I hadn't always been the most patient husband. I needed to improve by listening to Sophie more intently. When she asked me to reserve time to talk, I would snap, "Talk about what?" I already had an answer before she had finished the sentence. I considered her reasoning wimpy and of little significance to solve our underlying problems. Her arguments spun around in a vortex with no tangible solution.

More than solving a problem, Sophie wanted emotional support and my undivided attention in sharing her feelings. She was begging for understanding, sympathy, and love in a world that had become estranged to her. I should have said, "Now I understand how you feel. This must be difficult for you." I was a troubleshooter and repairman who could fix most electrical and mechanical problems but had little patience in sharing feelings, much less fixing them. Our emotional needs were miles apart. Each of us was looking for a different solution and finding no common ground.

God wired a man's brain differently from that of a woman's, and a husband needs to learn how to better understand the wife he married. Man likes predictability, order, and common sense, but God made women to bring color into a linear world. A man may be a simpler machine, but this is no excuse to shut down when a wife's suggestion sounds petty. Many times the woman is right and the man only begins seeing the deeper meaning later. A woman has abilities and intuitions that are often hidden from the man.

We often go through times of uncertainty when our vision is obscure. We stomp along, not knowing where the path will lead and where to turn. We worry what lies ahead and envision obstructions that block the road on our journey. And yet, we must march on. There is no lingering or surrendering because we have the children in tow. A hasty departure could cause more damage than living out the storm.

By welcoming Sophie back I tried to keep the flame of our marriage alive. I was ready to start from the beginning. No, I didn't expect a perfect marriage, but I wanted to do what was best for the family. I was willing to compromise for the sake of the children.

My intention was noble and right, but reality is harsh. It was a shock when it dawned on me that keeping an ailing marriage alive against all odds was not in the best interest of the family. It had been a mistake to take my wife back. What I thought were only bruises on the skin of the apple had caused the core to rot from the inside out. The marital problems began devouring the apple and the family started to collapse under its own weight.

In the following chapters we look at the effect an ailing marriage can have on the children. We address the critical duty of the responsible parent in taking corrective actions. Staying married may not always be the right answer.

The good spouse has little power when things go wrong. He or she is only one piece of the puzzle and cannot master the others. Goodwill and love do not save a marriage when the mind of the partner drifts.

CHAPTER 4

IMPACT ON THE CHILDREN

DEEP-ROOTED FAULT LINES

After Sophie moved back into the home, our relationship improved and I had great hope that our family life would become normal again. To fulfill her dream, we built a new house on the next-door lot that we had purchased earlier. We thought that a larger home would give us more comfort, and the four boys would no longer be cramped into one bedroom. The anticipated stability did not come, and soon after moving into the new house in early 1991, our family went into a free fall.

Sophie was now a full-time at home mom and missed her job as an accountant at the university. Doing "only" housekeeping duty was not her desired career and the state of the house reflected this. Our relationship became distant and she chose to sleep in a different room.

Meanwhile, Sophie decided to go for a routine medical examination. The family doctor knew about the nervous breakdown she had suffered one month earlier during our trip to California, and a sharp argument erupted between doctor and patient regarding the diagnosis. The doctor called me at work and said, "Sophie has a personality disorder; she will argue until she wins by using her intellectual powers to mask the problems within her." The doctor said further that her disorder is most difficult on the people closest to her, especially the spouse. She referred to other cases she knew about that caused family disruptions and led to divorce. The doctor hinted that sooner or later I wouldn't be able to cope with the stress of living with her anymore, that I could fall ill, or the family could break apart. She advised separation or divorce.

"You are a sick man and *you* should go see a doctor," Sophie yelled at me when I came home that evening. She was in a fighting mood and began accusing me of being an unfit father and a failure as a husband and provider. Not wanting to go back to the same doctor, she switched and chose a different physician in New Westminster.

Realizing Sophie's deteriorating mental state, I took off time from work and made several appointments with mental health organizations, explaining to the counselors the difficulty in raising a family with a mentally ill spouse. They were kind enough to listen but replied, "Unless your wife comes of her own accord, we cannot help." I then contacted the Royal Columbian Hospital, where Sophie had been treated, but the nurses released no information. Next, I made an appointment with Sophie's new doctor. The Filipina woman listened to me briefly and then said, "Sophie is a very gentle person and cultural differences may cause the problem." She then hinted that I might be too harsh with her. The doctor wasn't interested in her medical history and the treatment she had received.

I left the doctor's office with the guilty feeling of having betrayed my own wife by saying negative things about her. My face was burning with shame and I became a naughty little boy again, fearing having done something terribly wrong and wanting to escape. Nobody believed in me, and I felt like a thug who was trying to sell a product that no one dared to buy.

I had exhausted all avenues and there was nothing more I could do. I fell between the cracks of organizations that were unable, or unwilling, to reach out and help. Associations that could have offered assistance were family services, but I was not familiar with any of them. I was apprehensive about contacting government organizations, because I was worried that they might interfere with our family or, worse, take the children away.

Meanwhile at home, Sophie's illogical action began distorting the boundaries of what was right and wrong, and the children got confused.

Rewards and punishments were out of step with reality. A good shopping trip would bestow greater tolerance than doing mere housekeeping chores. The penalties were administered by Sophie's frame of mind and not by the severity of the misdemeanor.

Lack of discipline combined with poor parental guidance prompted the children to take off in an unpredictable way. It came as a shock to me when I learned that my own youngsters got involved in illegal activities outside the home. Police cruisers began appearing at the house. There were police arrests and summons to court.

I could not understand why my own children would suddenly turn a corner and stray from the moral upbringing we had instilled in them. It seemed as if I had lost control, and the values taught no longer applied. They took off in a wild and dangerous way.

The punishment administered by the civil authority appeared mild, and I reinforced it by using the rod. "I have to punish you," I told my son, and asked, "When do you want it?" He chose before going to bed that night. As he lay on his tummy, I first explained what type of penalty was coming. I then took the rod and slowly counted: one . . . two . . . three . . ., with each count striking the rod on his lower butt. I began softly and went a little harder with the subsequent strikes, but kept them measured. My son groaned, not knowing how much more was coming.

Both of us were relieved when the ordeal was over. I am certain that the mental pain was greater than the physical. He knew that he had earned it and accepted the penalty as a fair return. There was a sense of calm in the bedroom, and I used this teachable moment to remind him how far he can go, and not further. I tucked him into bed and we said a short prayer before turning off the light that night.

Blaming the bad behavior on parental ineptitude, the city authorities ordered Sophie and me to take counseling. After I explained the family situation, the counselor reckoned that Sophie was the cause of the trouble and urged me to divorce her. "I am a Christian and I believe in the power of prayer," I protested. "Divorce is not an option." At the conclusion of the six-session program, the counselor recommended divorce again, and I rejected the notion for the second time on the basis that it was biblically wrong.

I was naïve and should have taken the advice of the professional city counselor. Declining secular guidance and following a religious mandate alone caused the inevitable to happen. An earlier divorce would have been better, because the damage to my family occurred *before* the divorce and not as the result of it. This is also the belief of my grown children, who witnessed the disintegration of the family.

A 2005 study published in the *Journal of Marriage and Family*[a] supports this view. The report says, "Even before a marital breakup, young children of parents heading for divorce tend to develop mental health problems." Further studies originating from the *Research Data Centre*[b] and published in the *Journal of Marriage and Family* find that the demise of a marriage is most harmful to a child's mental health before a parental split, rather than after.[c] Researchers at the University of Alberta concluded that the common notion that parents should stay together for the sake of their kids is a fallacy that can do more harm to children than good.[d]

Not everybody supports this view. In her book *Between Two Worlds*, Elisabeth Marquardt disputes that children do better when parents separate. She writes that in case after case, children of divorce suffer more deeply and experience more emotional battles than children of intact families. She goes on to say that a divorce resulting from extreme circumstances is the exception. (From the book *Between Two Worlds* by Elisabeth Marquardt)

I agree with Marquardt's view in cases where two partners cannot get along for trivial reasons or self-inflicted causes. I call these "flu symptoms," superficial irritants that can mostly be resolved with goodwill, counseling, and prayer. Too many marriages break up as a result of pettiness or moral trespass. Marquardt refers to these self-inflicted divorces as "a good divorce," a term that suggests that a divorce will solve the family problems. It may not!

PAIN ON THE CHILDREN

In summer of 1991, Sophie initiated a new divorce. She was convinced that I was the cause of the family problems and gave the following reason for divorce: "My husband has caused the mental breakdown;

he has motivated the children to be against me, and he has failed to become a better person after I changed for the better." At one point, she wanted to keep the children, envisioning herself as a loving mother in a functional family, but after a hard day at home she was happy to pass them on to me.

I began worrying about the safety of the children. I noticed wounds that resembled fingernail marks on the children's faces, arms, and legs, and suspected physical abuse. Naturally, Sophie wouldn't admit to any wrongdoing, but it happened again and again, and the wounds looked fresh. I kept my suspicions under wraps in fear of the authorities apprehending the children.

Holly, then 16, got embroiled in many bitter fights with her mother. Rather than trying to calm the situation, as a wise parent should do, Sophie would provoke the children by throwing fuel into the fire. This did not go well with a teenager, and eventually Holly couldn't take it any longer and she moved out.

There we were, standing in the hallway, saying good-bye. Holly's bags were packed and her ride was waiting in front of the house. It was then that I noticed what a lovely young woman she had become. Even though her face was covered in tears, it radiated beauty. Her eyes yearned for love and kindness in a world she didn't understand. As I embraced the tall and slender body, her long hair got entangled in my arms and I began realizing how much we had missed each other. This beautiful daughter was now leaving. I choked and all I could utter was, "I am sorry."

Harsh fights also broke out between Sophie and Perry, then 13. If provoked, he would hit back really hard. He had a fierce temper and knew how to defend himself. I needed to step in many times to calm the situation.

Mattie, then ten, was affected the most by the abuse. He no longer cried when hurt, but went quietly to his bedroom, closed the door, and lay on his bed, his eyes empty and without emotion. He withdrew into his own world, and I couldn't comfort him. Communication was impossible. I felt sorry for Mattie because he was a nice, well-behaved boy. Being a compliant child made him an easy target. Mattie told me later that he was hiding in closets to escape the wrath of his mother.

When Todd, then eight, got hurt, he would cry profoundly and let the whole world know how miserable he felt. Perhaps this was the best approach. The superficial wounds that had been inflicted were brushed off. With my hug his smile would return. His big teary eyes would look up to me and find reassurance that the world was still a good place to live. Little Randy, then six, was spared physical abuse. He was our baby and was too cute and innocent to be hurt.

The children still needed their mom's loving care and received it generously during the good times. But love blended with unfair punishment produced a confusing mix. It was in December 1991 when little Todd surprised me with an unusual request. Looking at me with his big pleading eyes, he asked, "Dad, when can we get rid of Mamma?"

"Perhaps after Christmas," I said.

"No, Daddy," Todd insisted, "I want Mom to leave *before*, so we can have a happy Christmas." This made me realize how much the children were suffering and that a change was urgent.

Eight months had passed since Sophie's nervous breakdown, and life at home was more difficult than ever. For an outsider, a solution may appear simple: Call the police, contact Social Services, report the guilty party, and send the spouse away. This might work for a stranger but such treason would be a betrayal of the first degree for a spouse. I cannot imagine anyone going this far. Being of one flesh in marriage, as the Bible says, and then turning the spouse in would have gone against every grain in my body. I simply couldn't strike down my own wife, even though there was little affection between us and we were already mentally divorced.

The time was getting critical, and I needed to find an amicable and legal way to remove my wife from the home. This happened surprisingly quickly. While I was away in Japan on business, Holly visited her mother and a bitter fight erupted. Holly got hurt, called 911, and was admitted to the emergency room for treatment. As with all family disputes, the hospital reported the incident to Social Services.

Immediately, Social Services set up a time to see us. I was tight-lipped at the meeting because I didn't want government authorities entangling in our family affairs. Showing a good face, I tried to convince the counselors that I had everything under control and that things were improving. Not convinced of this, the counselors wanted to know more about our home life and kept asking questions. It was then when I explained that the incident between mother and daughter might have been an isolated case and blurted out that Sophie has now stopped hurting the children.

"Hurting the children?" the social worker shouted.

I knew right away that I had blown it. I'd said too much. My remarks hit like a lightning strike. Now the secret was out. When the social worker quizzed me further, I admitted sheepishly that, yes, I had a strong suspicion of physical abuse and that the children had been suffering. Social Services acted swiftly. Under the threat of apprehending the children, the authorities ordered the immediate removal of Sophie from the family home. Her sister picked her up the next day, only one hour short of the 24-hour deadline. Todd got his Christmas wish. Was it a happy Christmas? No, it was my worst.

Should I have reported the suspected child abuse to the authorities earlier? It is our legal obligation but most citizens would do as I did—keep quiet. A study by the Ontario Association of Children's Aid Societies (CACAS) suggests that nearly half of Ontarians would be hesitant to report child abuse. Citizens don't want to make the call for fear of retribution. Most lack understanding of what constitutes physical abuse. No one wants to be a whistle blower and everyone hopes that the problem will go away by itself.[e]

Sophie's departure closed a long and difficult chapter in our marriage. The uncertainty of who should leave the home was resolved. The wandering in the desert with no clear direction was over, and the fear of a family disaster was behind us. I had taken the long route and lived out the storm, but the problems weren't over. The mop-up had only begun. It was bigger and more difficult than I had anticipated.

LOOKING AFTER MYSELF FIRST

My oldest son had just pulled another stunt when I realized that something was seriously wrong with the home base. I saw my family falling further into an abyss with each day. Having become a single dad, my leadership was being tested. I had to focus on one thing alone—getting the family back on track before the authorities would take away this parental right. I needed to keep my mind as sharp as a player entering a chess competition, and my physical stamina as strong as an athlete running in the Olympics. Losing my composure for only a moment could have caused devastation.

As the children's illegal activities continued, I became alarmed and defensive. It was like a fuse that blows on overload when too many bad things go wrong all at once. I began seeing my intrinsic limitations and recognized that I had to look after myself first. The others would have to come second. I didn't do this out of neglect for the family, but for sheer self-preservation. I simply couldn't go on giving without replenishing myself. Running on empty with no energy to spare would have caused a disaster. A dead battery is of little use. It's nothing more than useless deadweight. As we learn to put on our oxygen mask before assisting others in preparation for takeoff, so also did I have to look after myself first to be able to help others, should the oxygen fail.

I began struggling with God. "How could You have allowed this to happen?" I cried out. "What have I done wrong?" Finally, one day, in total desperation, I handed the kids over to God and asked Him to look after them. I had done all I could. Now it was time for God to show if He was real and if He would help. After all, I had heard so many good things about Him and I was ready to test Him in my own way. If it failed, I would have someone to blame.

God must have heard my blunt and desperate prayer. The plan worked. After the separation and divorce, God provided me with new strength and wisdom to manage the family. With a steady dose of home discipline, the teenage aggressions began tapering off and the family became stable again. A calm arrived and life became meaningful, yes, even enjoyable. Police cruisers no longer stopped in front of our house and juvenile court hearings became a thing of the past.

Corrections and submission take time, and Will Durant[6] is right by saying, "From barbarism to civilization requires a century, from civilization to barbarism needs but a day." Destruction is easier than rebuilding, and giving free reign is simpler than taming and cultivating.

God assigns the job of disciplining the children to the parent(s). Woe, if the authorities must step in and finish this task in an institution! Motivational speaker Zig Ziglar[18] emphasizes the importance of home discipline with these famous words:

> The child who has not been disciplined with love by his little world will be disciplined, generally without love, by the big world. Real love demands that you do what is best for your child, not necessarily what your child wants you to do, or what is easiest for you.
>
> —Zig Ziglar

When Sophie and I took the preparation courses at our church before getting married, I had never imagined that a family could fall this low. Nor did I know how little control I had to stop the plunge. I went by the teaching, "For whatever a man sows, that he will also reap," and I was determined to sow good seed. The sample cases that were presented to us as teaching material now looked like schoolboy stuff. The lessons were exclusively based on the assumption that both partners were reasonable. Love, communication, and forgiveness were taught as the main negotiation tools in solving marital disputes. But what choice does one have when reasoning and common sense no longer prevail? What should the good spouse do if the partner turns into a monster?

Marriage preparation courses do not address *divorce for just cause*, a situation in which a marriage *must* be dissolved to regain personal dignity and respect. I can see why instructors conceal unusual circumstances at these courses, for fear of scaring new couples away from entering a lifelong covenant.

Marriage and family form a strong union; spousal misconduct tears it apart. Building a happy family takes precedence over marriage. Clear guidance from one parent is better than two in conflict.

CHAPTER 5

PAIN OF DIVORCE

DIVORCE FOR JUST CAUSE

Marriage is built on the understanding that both parties are reasonable. Many marriages suffer from fundamental flaws that cannot be resolved. A spouse having a personality disorder or a mental infirmity is such an example. When discussing *divorce for just cause*, we are talking about marriages that do not function, cannot be fixed, and damage the nucleus of the family if allowed to continue.

After the nervous breakdown, the hospital recommended that Sophie and I take marriage counseling. I was hesitant to engage in such an exercise. I knew that this would only work if both parties were reasonable and willing to change. As anticipated, the counseling was a waste of time and money. Although based on Christian principles, the counselor ignored the root problem and followed the goal of reuniting husband and wife, regardless of the cause. I wanted him to assume a leadership role, take examples from other marriages with mental illness, and base the decision on known facts. This didn't happen and we canceled the sessions after six months with no positive result.

I continued seeking advice by seeing my parish priest. He was well connected with behavioral problems in marriage and understood my family responsibility. To explain the severity of my situation in greater detail, I handed him a copy of *My Story*, a twenty-page journal in which I had recorded the events as they unfolded during our troubled marriage. Without hesitation, the priest advised me to go ahead with the divorce. In a stern voice he said, "Pull through to the bitter end, even if the going gets rough. Don't look back." This advice helped me get through the difficult divorce proceedings that soon followed. At about this time, my family doctor called to say that continuing the relationship could affect my mental and physical health, and recommended separation or divorce.

I took the advice of these two professionals to heart, mustered my courage, and signed the divorce papers that Sophie's lawyer had prepared for me. It may strike the reader odd that Sophie was the petitioner. I believe that her eagerness to get rid of me was connected to her mental illness. She was convinced that I was the cause of our family problems. In her eyes, I was an evil man.

THE DECISION TO DIVORCE FALLS ON YOU

Stepping out of a long-term marriage is a serious undertaking, and before signing the divorce papers I asked my Christian friends for advice. I had known Frank and Mary for many years and respected their opinion. What surprised me was their strong opposition to divorce, even though they knew my difficult family situation. Frank said point-blank, "Your wife has given you five children, and now that she is ill and needs your support you want to dump her like a used tea bag!" He reminded me that marriage is an irrevocable union, ordained by God for the benefit of husband and wife, a partnership that cannot be broken by illness. Marriage is for life.

His words struck like lightning and I was reminded again of my immutable obligation to my wife as husband and protector, especially now that she was ill. I thought I had done my homework and divorce was simply a matter of signing the legal papers. She wanted it and I had a family to raise. Frank's position made me rethink my options and I started asking: "Am I moving against God's will to destroy something that the Lord wants me to keep? Is this a test from God to examine my integrity?"

Guilt feelings collided with a need to find a solution. Moral conduct—a code dominated by emotional and religious qualities—fought with common sense, reminding me of my parental duty toward the children. My emotions seesawed in a most disturbing way, fluttering like a flag in the wind, not knowing which direction to take. Abandoning the divorce would have been easy, but this route had been tried before and failed. Nothing had changed that would warrant a change in my plan. Meanwhile, the family was being crushed under its own weight and we could no longer carry on.

In a state of confusion, I asked God for guidance and spent time on my knees. Prayer helped set the priorities, detached from emotions and the religious bondage that often distort the thinking at a time of trial. I believe that prayer guided me to the right decision by realizing that my ultimate duty was (and still is) directed toward the family.

I always held a deep spiritual reverence for marriage. The promise to stay together in sickness and in health was still fresh in my mind. I remembered Sophie clinging to me and with teary eyes begging, "Don't ever leave me!" I recalled the dreams she had, seeing me riding away on a white horse and disappearing in the dusk, never to come back again. I recalled my solemn promise to her, saying, "I will never leave you." As important as these pledges were, I began shifting toward the welfare of the children and realized that divorce was the only sensible solution. The family came first.

I knew I couldn't please all parties involved and picked the path of least destruction. By choosing divorce, I purposely broke my wedding vow, disregarded the teaching of the church, and ignored the advice of my Christian friends. I took the advice given by my doctor who knew our circumstances and had seen similar cases leading to disaster if allowed to continue. I also accepted the counsel of the parish priest, who was aware of the harm an untenable family situation can bring. He spoke to me as the *shepherd* of his flock and not as a church authoritarian.

Most marriages torn by debilitating mental or behavioral problems will eventually dissolve. Reconciliation is almost impossible, and the "when" rests on how long the spouse can hang on. Engaging in counseling and seeking a reunion seldom works for the long haul, and the on-again, off-again relationship causes more harm to the family than a finite state.

The notion that all marriages can be saved with goodwill and dedication is incorrect, and we should not be so naive as to seek reconciliation when a solution is not feasible. *The health of the family must come first* and rigid religious rules cannot stand in the way. If a divorce is inevitable, such interference will only confuse the issue further and inflict additional harm to an already hurting family.

Churches and religious leaders must respect divorce as an *immutable human right* on which to draw when other options are not workable. Nowhere does the Bible say that we must stay in an unworkable marriage. God is less concerned about breaking rules than achieving inner peace. Being miserable by sticking it out in an unworkable marriage is not His plan. The gift of life is too precious. Jesus knew about this and was careful in giving answers on divorce when asked. We read in John 14:27, "Peace I leave with you; my peace I give you. I do not give to you as the world gives. Do not let your hearts be troubled and do not be afraid."

I have met many devout couples who were very dedicated to marriage, spoke about its insolvency at group meetings, and wrote extensively on this topic. Then mental illness struck and the couple could no longer live together. Divorce reestablished dignity and allowed the healthy parent to raise the children in a functional home setting, albeit alone. I've also met couples who entered marriage very casually. "We'll try and see if it works for us," they say, as if doing a social experiment. Many years later, these couples are still happily married and raising obedient kids.

DIVORCE VS. DEATH

When divorce knocks on the door with no other way out, reality strikes and the mood gets somber. We had been married for twenty years, raised a large family, and built a business together. The divorce created a major setback; it was the end of a way of life that was so precious to us. I cannot think of a better-fitting metaphor than comparing divorce with *death*. When divorce became inevitable with no other way out, I prayed that God would take either one of us in death, and I was prepared to depart should I be the chosen one.

A divorce goes through similar stages of acceptance as death. In her book *On Death and Dying,* the late Dr. Elisabeth Kubler-Ross[12] describes the five stages as *denial, anger, bargaining, depression and yearning,* and *acceptance.*

I remember having gone through all of these stages, beginning with *denial.* For a long time I covered up the difficulties, and we were viewed as a well-functioning and happy couple—and we were. We went to church together and received many compliments in restaurants on how well the children behaved (sometimes). We were seen as a role model, and our friends living in a common-law relationship married on account of our good marriage. When divorce was imminent I expressed deep anger and asked myself, "Will I be able to keep the house and the company, or will I need to start from scratch again?" Anger led to *plea-bargaining* and I tried reconciling with Sophie one more time. I visited medical institutions, had lengthy discussions with my Christian friends, and agreed to take marriage counseling. When a workable solution was unreachable, I felt the onslaught of *helplessness* and *depression.* I stopped caring for my wife and considered our marriage a lost cause. She turned away from me and started sleeping in a different bedroom. Observing how well other families were doing, I began *yearning* for a functional marriage again and prayed more intently than ever, only to be led to the slaughterhouse and crushed in the end. I began questioning the goodness of God and became skeptical about religion and the church. I discontinued reading the Bible and stopped doing family devotions. I went through a spiritual descent and distanced myself from the church. Nothing made sense anymore. I finally *accepted* and *surrendered* to the divorce.

Breaking up a once-successful marriage is one of the most agonizing trials a human must endure. Helen Richards, a survivor of a Nazi concentration camp, knew this and articulated the pain endured because of her divorce when she spoke at a women's retreat in 1985. She said:

> My husband announced that he was leaving. This was one of my hardest things I ever had to cope with. I just could not understand. We were married for 24 years. Why would God bring me out of this for that? It's hard to make a comparison between Hitler's concentration camp and divorce. To me,

that was worse than the concentration camp had ever been. In the concentration camp, I was young. It was not personal, but I wanted to survive. But this time, I wanted to die. My heart hurt. I was afraid.

Helen Richards grew up in the former Soviet Union and went through unbelievable hardship during Word War II. The Nazis executed her brother; she was put in an extermination camp, witnessed the execution of 50,000 people, and smelled the smoke from the ovens that burned the bodies. Miraculously, she survived and moved to the U.S., where she married.

When Helen said that divorce was worse than the concentration camp, she underscored the meaning of "being one flesh," flesh that had been ripped off her bones. She got over the childhood drama but could not take the marriage breakup. Being disrespected and dumped by the husband she loved was harder to endure than the Nazi repression. Scars inflicted in childhood tend to flush off more easily than if received in the adult life. Youth offers hope but afflictions suffered in adulthood wound the body permanently.

A few years ago a strange incident happened in our neighborhood. Two women lost their husbands, one to death and the other to divorce. The divorcee uttered to the grieving widow, "Aren't you lucky that your husband died?" The widow was stunned and didn't know what to say. "Lucky?" she protested, "We had a good marriage." The divorced woman simply wanted to express how much more dignified death was than divorce.

When asked, "What is harder to take, divorce or death?," most would say death. Yet those who have experienced a difficult divorce will agree with me that divorce is the tougher one. Let me hasten to say that I'm not qualified to make judgment between the two. We all think that our suffering is unique and that no one would understand the depth of anguish. God does. He knows our thinking and shares in the pain. Jesus Christ suffered more than any of us ever will when He died on the cross. He did this to show His love for us and to grant salvation.

Comparing divorce with death as a measure of pain is a very sensitive subject that needs to be handled with great care and in the right context. Nevertheless, I am taking this liberty, and in so doing I'm breaking the stigma that divorce is self-inflicted and death is God-ordained. In fairness to the comparison, we assume that both losses are unavoidable and no one is to blame. After all, we are all guilty in the eyes of God. We all have broken God's law, whether we're single, married, or divorced.

What makes a divorce so heartbreaking is the human suffering that precedes the breakup. The stressful situation of living with an estranged spouse will already have taken its toll and caused serious mental and physical trauma before the divorce occurred. This could be accusations, lies, demeaning comments, and physical abuse. Take an adulterous partner, for example, who continues with transgressions without remorse. The spirit of the spouse is destroyed and divorce comes as a relief from the silent torture. It becomes a victory over suffering. Mopping up the last spillover is easier to take than living with the stench of a sewer that continuously overflows.

I don't want to diminish the grief of losing a loved one. This is a devastating tragedy that cuts deeply into the fabric of our personal lives and paralyzes the family. But the social implication of death is kinder and more humane than divorce. Death carries no stigma. It has no victim. It was God's wise plan to call the loved one home. Children cope better in a finite state, and in most cases the family remains stable. The explanation that Mommy or Daddy is in heaven works better than confronting a parent who shows resentment and neglects the children with infrequent visits or interferes with the upbringing. In this respect, the grave is a friendlier place than the custody battle.

At a funeral, only the good deeds of the deceased person are remembered. The negative ones are left unspoken, buried in the grave. The church community offers the grieving family support. Prayers are said and sympathy is poured out. The women of the church get together, prepare food, provide housekeeping chores, and offer babysitting. Such outreach conveys a deep respect and human dignity.

At a divorce hearing in a courtroom the tone is different. There are no consoling words for the hurting couple. Instead of sympathy the lawyers haggle over trivial events and make accusations against each other to reach a better settlement. There is lashing and whipping as if these two hurting spouses were convicted criminals. The Christian community is far removed from this ordeal and does not respond. A pastor would not visit the court chambers as he does the sickroom in the hospital. There are no rituals to assist divorced couples coping with the grief.

The lack of outreach from the church community inflicts serious damage on divorcees and the children. I have experienced this in my own family. After the separation and divorce, my children began disputing God and Christian values in a worrisome way. They stopped going to church and became skeptical about religion. It took years to recover. A helping hand would have softened the pain and made the wounds heal quicker.

A study by the University of Texas in Austin reveals that the experience of a divorce makes children less religious than peers from intact families.[a] A separate survey commissioned by the PBS television network found that a wide gulf forms between religious teachings on the sanctity of marriage and reality. The pain of seeing their parents divorce causes many children to conclude that God cannot be trusted. Moreover, many Christians never set foot in a church again after a difficult divorce.

I encourage the church community to make a greater effort in reaching out to single parents and the children to help them cope with the loss and to bring them back to the church community. I realize that it's easier to distance oneself from a divorced family than to help. Pointing fingers and blaming the couple for the demise reflects a lack of compassion and understanding. This is opposite of what Jesus taught and what the Bible says.

I remember reaching out to members of my church and received little in support during my struggles. I was disappointed but understood that people want to stay at a safe distance. They are hesitant to get involved in someone's personal affairs, especially in a divorce, because there are always two sides to a story. Good help is hard to find; gossip is more common, and the person needing support is often left alone.

A divorce creates other obstacles, one of which is the custody of the children. I feel deep sadness for the parent who goes empty-handed. It is with overwhelming disappointment that a parent can no longer care for the children and be at their side when they ask for help.

As if the custody struggle were not enough, the family resources must be split and the legal bills paid. Studies at Ohio State University's Center for Human Resource Research report that couples who divorced lost on average 77 percent of their personal net worth.[b] In death, these assets are kept in the family and the surviving spouse becomes the sole owner of them. The widow may also be the beneficiary of a life insurance policy, a welcome contribution that sustains the family when losing the breadwinner. Such monetary contribution is not bestowed on a divorcee. There is no such thing as marriage insurance.

COURT HEARINGS

During our lengthy divorce preparations, the engagement ring came up again. Sophie said that it was lost and the court accepted her claim. After the divorce, the ring miraculously reappeared and she sold it for good money.

I also learned that Sophie had spent far more money on personal items than I had anticipated. "How could she spend all this money in such a short time?," I demanded, to which her lawyer replied, "These are the facts; she had a right to the funds, and nothing more can be done about it." The court accepted her lavish spending and said, "One needs to keep up the lifestyle to which one is accustomed." The court did not associate the uncontrolled spending habits with her mental illness.

I recommend that couples who are going through a divorce set limits on spending. This is especially important if one partner tries to take advantage of the situation and overspends to avoid sharing the assets. Precious cash could quickly evaporate, draining the much-needed seed money to kick-start the family after the divorce. Most lawyers are only concerned with getting the job done and receiving the legal fees. They are less interested in the family's financial stability after the divorce.

Sophie's medical condition caused many delays, and in March 1994, after a three-year wait, the court hearings finally began in earnest. There I was, sitting in the courtroom, anxiously waiting for the judge to arrive. The mood was somber, our faces were overcome with sadness, and the few visitors who arrived were equally gloomy-faced. I couldn't face my in-laws and looked the other way when they drew close.

Gazing around the courtroom I saw a parallel between the courtroom and the Jewish temple of the Old Testament. There was what appeared to be an elevated altar in the front—the "holy-of-holies"—where the high priest resided in olden days. In this present setting the area was reserved for the judge. One step lower was a specially designated spot for the priests, now occupied by lawyers who had already assembled. And then there was the gallery at the back of the room where the common people gathered. This was our assigned area. A railing separated the gallery from the theatre. A similar partition can still be seen in medieval churches where commoners gather behind a massive iron gate to hear Mass. The Vatican Council II (1962–1965) changed this practice and brought the church into the 20th century, and beyond.

Although the physical layout may show a similarity between a church and a court, I soon learned that the services provided are diametrically opposed to each other. In the church the altar represents the place where we bring our transgressions to God for forgiveness and salvation. God opens His arms and invites us in, and then forgives our trespasses. He bestows His blessings on us and we depart with *hope, faith,* and *love*. In court, the altar resembles the bench on which the judge reigns with absolute authority. *Woe to the guilty!* Rather than being forgiven, the judge inflicts a penalty and sends the guilty away to fend for himself.

The judge finally arrived and we were asked to stand. After a brief introduction, the hearings began. As petitioner, Sophie was asked to take the witness stand first. With the help of her skilled lawyer, her answers were well delivered, brief, and complete. Observing her from the gallery I was again reminded of her calm and collected mannerism, qualities that had attracted me to her when we first met in church. My mind drifted back to our wedding day. I saw Sophie walking down the church aisle in her long white dress. She had adorned herself and looked incredibly beautiful. Her eyes sparkled and her complexion was radiant like the sun. Walking toward me, she smiled, and hand in hand we walked up to the altar. Our hearts overflowed with joy and excitement. We promised to stay together in sickness and in health until death do us part. The priest gave us a blessing and symbolically bound us together with a rope to make us "one flesh."

After finishing the questions on the stand, Sophie was asked to go back to her seat. She avoided eye contact as she walked by. She had her people; I had mine. The lawyers told us to refrain from verbal exchange. All communication had to go through them. What a contrast this was to our wedding day!

Throughout the hearings I had the support of my friend Frank. Every morning he was waiting for me in the lobby of the Vancouver Courthouse in downtown Vancouver. Together we went up to the assigned courtroom and he sat through the entire trial. Sometimes his wife Mary would also join us. I later learned that Frank had taken his vacation to be at my side. *We are never alone. God sends helpers when the going gets rough.*

During the strenuous eight days in court I felt as if I had lost a personal battle and was being punished for having done something terribly wrong. How else would one end up in court and be ruled by a judge? Tearing our marriage apart was a heartrending experience because deep inside we still loved each other. I lost the woman I had always wanted. I called out to God, but He was not there. At moments like this one can only cry out as Jesus did on the cross, "My God, my God, why have you forsaken me?" (Matt. 27:46).

Feeling disconnected from God is part
of Christian life, and we are not alone.
Romans 5:3-4 reminds us: "We rejoice
in our sufferings, because we know
that suffering produces perseverance;
perseverance character; and character
hope." The wisdom gained is deep and
beyond our understanding.

CHAPTER 6

BUSINESS AND DIVORCE

STARTING MY OWN BUSINESS

Mental illness not only devastates the family; it makes running a jointly owned business virtually impossible. In this concluding chapter of Part One we go back in time and experience how my wife's illness distressed our newly formed family business. Infirmity is a serious matter under all circumstances, but if it strikes the co-owners of a growing enterprise, then the challenges become insurmountable. This happened to us.

I had always dreamed of running my own business. I was full of creative ideas and wanted to do more than settle for an ordinary nine-to-five job. While working at General Electric, I realized that the rechargeable battery for two-way radios caused many field failures. This led me to develop a battery analyzer that could test these batteries. During my research I discovered a way to rejuvenate nickel-cadmium batteries. I took the idea home, pooled the family savings, and developed a battery analyzer that featured the innovative "recondition" cycle.

So thrilled was I about my discovery that I dreamed of instant success. This didn't happen. Although the device worked well, I sold only a few of the first-generation battery analyzers. I lacked manufacturing and marketing experience and thought that a useful product would sell on its own merit. This was far from reality.

The setback did not discourage me and I started to develop a modular battery analyzer that would adapt to many different battery types, not just the packs from GE. The new model sold better and the company made a small profit in 1983. We moved the operation from our house into a rented office and set up a legal company under the name of Cadex Electronics Inc. Sophie and I were equal shareholders. I appreciated her accounting expertise and her keenness in proofreading my correspondence. She was excited about the plans to expand the company and supported me fully.

But then suddenly, without reason, she put her foot down and opposed my ideas. I was unable to figure out her thinking pattern, and running the business turned into begging for approval on trivial things rather than using my own good judgment.

Anyone starting a business understands the ups and downs. Getting new orders is a thrilling experience and the excitement has no bounds. But then there are times of uncertainty when the apparent success begins to wane. This happened to us during the mid-1980s, when all orders dried up and our cash flow became tight.

To save money we let our housekeeper go and I began working from home again. My workshop soon became the preferred hangout for the kids and they often were careless while playing. Several times a swinging broom handle ripped down my delicate electronic experiments and I had to build the bird's nest of wires again. Once, the circuits went up in smoke.

I remember the difficulty talking with my customers over the phone with kids making noise in the background. I would wait until the house got quiet for a moment, and then quickly sneak up to my bedroom to make the calls. When the children noticed my absence, they came searching for me, shouting, "Daddy . . . Daddy . . . Daddy!" I wondered what the customers thought about my business!

We finally shipped the last analyzer and had no new orders in the book. "Should I look for a new job?" my co-worker asked. I answered, "No, stay. More orders will be coming." He stayed and we both began worrying. This was the time when I started praying. After the staff left for the day, I kneeled by my desk and ask our Good Lord to send orders to save the company.

And then an amazing thing happened: a company called out of the blue and offered funds to develop a microprocessor-controlled battery charger for an industrial application. The project was a success and we delivered more units than originally anticipated. The design of the charger later formed the foundation for other products. The company was saved.

LETTING SOPHIE GO

No longer employed at the university, Sophie began working full-time at Cadex as an accountant. Until then, her odd conduct had been confined to our home, but it began spilling over to the office. The female staff soon began complaining that Sophie had made unfair accusations against them. During the course of these events, the bank called to say that they urgently needed to see me. Three well-dressed officials arrived at the office to express grave concern about the company's financial management. I learned that Sophie had visited the bank several times to negotiate new loans. Instead of lending more money, the bank froze our line of credit and threatened to recall the existing loan. Sophie had good intentions of raising new capital, but her manner revealed her mental condition and the bank got concerned.

With the line of credit frozen we needed to find a new lending institution, and we did this without Sophie's help. Being excluded from an important business decision did not go over well and she took her frustration out on me. This left me with no other option than to release her from duty. With the help of a lawyer I called a board of directors meeting and voted her out of office.

The firing caused our already strained marital relationship to take a turn for the worse. Being in denial, she accused me of destroying her career and robbing her of an income. The in-laws were equally appalled at my action and my popularity hit rock bottom again.

Letting Sophie go was hard because she had played a pivotal role in the start-up phases. I had hoped that we could continue growing the company together but this was no longer feasible. Starting a business with the support of a spouse is one of the most rewarding endeavors a husband and wife can do. The satisfaction comes from hiring staff and caring for them, united as a couple. There is deep gratification in providing a source of income for workers with spouses who also raise children. I deeply regretted that we could no longer share this responsibility together.

Sophie's departure meant a new beginning for Cadex. I was now free to run the company on my own intuition. The new bank loaned us fresh money that we used for machinery, systems software, and new product design. The programmable battery analyzer introduced in 1991 was the right product at the right time. It played a pivotal role in capturing the lucrative cell phone market.

Cadex continued to grow and we relocated to larger premises many times, doubling plant size with each move. At first, the new place looked empty and out of place. Items that had been within arm's reach now required long-distance running to retrieve. Eventually, employees and equipment would fill in the space and the echoing sound of an empty manufacturing plant would be replaced with the hum of activity. I felt proud walking down the long corridors with offices to the left and right, filled with dedicated staff, serving customers and taking orders. We received a contract from a U.S. defense organization to supply battery chargers and analyzers for critical missions abroad. Another large order came from a leading medical company that treats cardiac arrests.

TURNING POINT

And then the inevitable happened—the divorce. The marriage break-up of company owners is bound to have a profound ripple effect in the business community. Greedy sharks soon invaded our offices, looking for their spoils. Anticipating Cadex's demise, a mischievous employee offered to buy the company and put it on the Vancouver Stock Exchange. I fired the man on the spot, but the plot had leaked into court and complicated the divorce hearings.

Sophie's relapses caused several reschedules of the court hearing. Before each appearance the lawyers demanded a reassessment of the company. Not only was this expensive, I could see the value of Cadex going up by 20 to 30 percent per year. Although that was good on its own, I worried that purchasing Sophie's 50 percent share would move beyond my reach.

In court, I expressed my desire to become sole owner of the company. The judge was indifferent to the idea and at the slightest disagreement on ownership issues he suggested that the company should be sold. This worried me and I made every attempt to cooperate. *What does a judge know about the inner workings of a business*, I thought? *How could a 'black robe' make an intelligent decision of what's best for the company? A careless move could easily destroy years of hard work and put the workers on the street.*

At the end, the court obliged and allowed me to buy my wife's shares. To make the purchase possible, I put everything I owned on the table. This was the second time in my life that I invested all I had into a high-risk venture. The first endeavor was kick-starting the company. Now I needed to buy back Sophie's share and I was prepared to take this risk.

The court then divided the remaining family assets, which included furniture and the piano, and assigned me as the custodian of the children. To my great relief, the judge allowed us to stay in the family home for the next ten years. At the expiry, the house was to be liquidated and half of the proceeds given to Sophie for additional compensation.

Relieved but financially broke, I began worrying how I could meet my family obligations that included a housekeeper and Christian education. In addition to these fixed expenses, the court ordered me to make monthly maintenance payments to support Sophie because she was unable to hold a job.

The shrewd action of the court enticed me to take equally harsh measures with my company. As sole owner I was determined to succeed. Perhaps it was out of sheer survival instinct that I fired five managers. I felt that the current administration was not capable of bringing Cadex to the next level, and I began with a major restructuring.

The reorganization worked and the new management team improved efficiency by slashing the 14-week delivery in half, eliminating low-margin products, streamlining operations by reducing redundant staff in some departments, and adding more in others. The programmable Cadex battery analyzer that we had developed served the market well and soon became the company's flagship, establishing a new standard to which competitive products were compared. The annual revenue grew to double digits and Cadex products were soon used in more than 100 countries.

It so happened that I was selected as a finalist for the Entrepreneur of the Year Award. To celebrate this prestigious event, I invited my family members and staff to the grand reception at the Pan Pacific Convention Center in downtown Vancouver. There I stood shoulder-to-shoulder with other entrepreneurs who had also succeeded in their endeavors. Perhaps my guests enjoyed the ceremony more than I did. Walking on stage in front of bright lights, TV cameras, and an applauding audience was not my favorite pastime activity. Everyone looked good in the dark suits and tuxedos, but overhearing other candidates talking behind the curtains made me realize I was in wrong company. No, I didn't own a boat, nor did I play golf in the afternoons and take vacations in exotic places. I was just a humble servant who had built a business on a shoestring.

After a few more years of rapid growth we were in a financial position to build our own headquarters. I acquired one of the most scenic parcels of land in a new industrial park on the Fraser River in Richmond, BC. The architect drew up the plans and I spent several months optimizing the floor layout and enhancing the appearance. Today, the building includes a large, two-story glass octagon that serves as entrance lobby and accommodates the reception and several meeting rooms. A broad staircase leading to the second floor portrays an atmosphere of grandeur and space. Balconies to the south of the building overlook the mighty Fraser River. During breaks, the staff enjoys watching the swans frolicking in the waters and the ducks grazing on the riverbanks.

On our grand opening in May 1999, representatives traveled from all corners of the world to partake at this celebration. During our dinner on a yacht while cruising in the scenic harbors of Vancouver, we experienced one of the most beautiful sunsets. This was a greeting card—an approval from God to us, saying, "Well done, good and faithful servant! You have been faithful with a few things; I will put you in charge of many things. Come and share your master's happiness" (Matt. 25:23).

Looking back and thinking about the positive changes that had occurred since my divorce, I could not help but thank the Lord for what He had done. Help from above was evident every step of the way. It was as if He had given me a stamp of approval and wanted to compensate for the unfortunate mishaps of the past. I had pedaled against headwinds all my life, or so it seemed. I remembered my high school teacher saying that I didn't measure up, my boss hinting that I wouldn't achieve anything in life, and even my dad expressing his doubt in my abilities. Establishing a new life in Canada was harder than I had imagined. With little English and lacking social skills, I couldn't achieve what came easy and natural for others. Interesting jobs were only a pipe dream and promotions got passed on to others. Marriage gave me a boost, but all too soon divorce knocked on the door.

As hard as these years may have been, they were a blessing in disguise. Had everything worked out as planned, I would not have started the company. Deep in my heart I knew that I could do it, and the roughing up gave me determination to persevere. We achieve by overcoming adversity. If we attain our goals too easily, we might drop the gift, break it in pieces, and tread it underfoot.

Moving ahead with full vigor I began overtaking career seekers who had run in front of me. I had the pleasure of welcoming many former employers and business owners to the new headquarters. One of them was a manager who had interviewed me for a job opening but decided not to hire me. I used to look up to these towering figures in trembling fear and utter respect—now we were equals. In humble recognition the words of Mark 10:31 came to mind: "Many who are first shall come last and the last shall come first."

Celebrating milestones are exciting moments, but I get uneasy when someone gives me flattering accolades for accomplishments to which I'm not fully entitled. I brush off such praises, thinking that these folks don't know any better. It's ironic that the reward system is entirely focused on a secular viewpoint in praising the person to whom help is given and ignoring the *Giver* who made it possible. St. Teresa of Avila[1] inspires us to think that we are a tool of the Lord. She writes:

> Christ has no body now on earth but yours, no hands but yours, no feet but yours; yours are the eyes through which Christ's compassion looks out on the world, yours are the

feet with which He is to go about doing good, and yours are the hands with which He is to bless us now.

—Saint Teresa of Avila

REPAYING WHAT THE LOCUSTS HAVE EATEN

The success of my business eventually brought a financial freedom that we couldn't enjoy before. Material wealth can be very satisfying, especially if earned with integrity, but this new freedom requires restraint. I continued to show moderation toward my children by giving an example of a simple lifestyle. I wanted to teach them the enduring value of money sincerely earned. This moderation also extends to my staff. I reflect this by commuting to work by bicycle whenever the circumstances permit.

Newly acquired fame and wealth often harm the delicate fabric of a family. Finding the right balance when prosperity strikes is often more difficult to handle than continuing with the struggle to make ends meet. Wealth quickly attained does not reflect on who we are as people. It does not provide lasting happiness, but encourages greed because the obtained status is in discord with our character and moral fiber. Only riches gained in sincerity through honest and hard work have staying power and provide satisfaction. Character and wealth must go hand in hand and harmonize. If not, one or both will slip away and be lost. It's harder to keep a full cup from spilling than one that is only half full.

Before God could give me financial freedom, He pried open my fist and took all I had earned in my "previous life." It was hard to let go and I complained bitterly. Like Job in the Bible, I needed to surrender the old before God could give the new. In the end, the biblical promise of Joel 2:25 was being fulfilled before my very eyes: "I will repay you for the years the locusts have eaten." Seeing the ruins being rebuilt was one of the most exhilarating experiences in my life.

One of my favorite Bible texts is the Prayer of Jabez. It portrays in very simple words the desire for mankind in wanting to expand and grow. I made several copies of the prayer, framed them, and placed them on the walls in my company and at home. The prayer reads:

Jabez cried out to the God of Israel, "Oh, that you would bless me and enlarge my territory! Let your hand be with me, and keep me from harm so that I will be free from pain." And God granted his request.

—1 Chronicles 4:10

To this prayer, I add:

Oh Lord, that You would give Cadex the wisdom and strength to carry out the work for the glory of God and the benefit of mankind; that You would continue to bless us; that You would send good workers to the harvest, and that You would protect us from greed and corruption.

Our life is a journey in understanding God's plan for us. He gives encouragement in knowing that we can conquer arduous times with willpower, determination, and perseverance. Accepting our destiny brings hope, healing, and inner peace. "With God, all things are possible" (Matthew 19:26).

PART II

SURRENDER AND ACCEPTANCE

Photo by Michael A. Wollen, www.mindtapmedia.com

CHAPTER 7

TEST OF FAITH

My conservative upbringing in the small village of Römerswil (near Lucerne, Switzerland) instilled in me a strong commitment to honesty and integrity. We had a strong Christian heritage—my grandmother prayed for us from the day we were born. Her sister was a nun in a convent who also prayed nonstop. Our circle of relatives included a Jesuit and a priest. As far as I could go back, there was no divorce in our family. Marriage was meant to be for life. So adamant was I about the permanency of marriage that I made derogatory hints to those who had divorced. I realize now that these remarks were insincere and I apologize.

Sophie also came from a devout Christian family. The proverb "Love is a decision" formed the foundation for our marriage. These words were engraved in our hearts at the two Marriage Encounter Weekends we attended.

Given this background, it is not surprising that going through a divorce, an act I so despised, made me question God's grace. "Was not marriage the very institution that God had given to mankind for the benefit of the family?" I asked. "Why then would the Good Lord not save my marriage? Was not marriage the very sacrament that God had intended to symbolize the relationship between Christ and His church?"

STRUGGLE WITH GOD

My spiritual questioning would have been less intense had it not been for the many prayers I said to save our marriage. Throughout our married life, and especially during the final years together, we prayed as husband and wife. I put my hand on Sophie's head and asked God for healing. *The healing did not come.* During moments of reconciliation and marriage renewal, we promised each other to try harder and hoped that through the power of forgiveness, God would give our marriage a new beginning and bestow His grace upon us. *The grace did not come.* Until the day of our separation, I urged God to intervene, perform a miracle, and save our marriage. *The help did not come.* When Social Services removed Sophie from the family, my last hope evaporated. Although the departure was a relief for all of us, it triggered a turning point in my spiritual life. Searching the Bible for answers, I read:

> Ask and you shall receive; seek and you shall find; knock and it shall be opened to you. For whoever asks, receives, whoever seeks, finds; whoever knocks, is admitted. What father among you will give his son a snake if he asks for a fish or hand him a scorpion if he asks for an egg? If you, with all your sins, know how to give your children good things, how much more will the heavenly Father give the Holy Spirit to those who ask him.
>
> —Luke 11:9–13 NAB

It was this very verse that triggered my spiritual collapse. After fervently asking God for help—and being denied—I could no longer contain my anger and considered the promises in the Bible as nothing more than empty fables. In a fury of madness, I grabbed the Book and with great force threw it against the wall. "Who can believe that stuff?" I cried. "Empty promises at best."

Until then, I believed that every word written in the Bible was a promise from God to mankind. I took the teaching at face value and expected results. As the divorce moved closer to reality and the children got involved in illegal activities, I wondered why such promises were recorded if they didn't work. After all, I asked for a fish and got a snake; I wanted an egg and received a scorpion. I felt the very God, in whom I had put my full faith, could no longer be trusted. The long walks in the evening, when I was in communications with God, turned into questioning if He even existed.

I finally picked up the wounded book from the floor and parked it on a shelf, this time for good. The pages crumpled but the binding stayed intact. I'm glad that the book held fast because I had made many worthwhile notes during my fifteen years of Scripture reading.

The late Mother Teresa also struggled spiritually. Her secret letters reveal that she spent most of her years without sensing the presence of God and wrote, "Where is my faith? Even deep down there is nothing but emptiness and darkness. If there be a God, [then] please forgive me . . . I am told God lives in me—and yet the reality of darkness, coldness, and emptiness is so great that nothing touches my soul . . . I want God with all the power of my soul, and yet between us there is terrible separation . . . I feel just that terrible pain of loss, of God not wanting me, of God not being God, of God not really existing."

During this time of struggle, a woman of the Sikh religion gave me a shroud with the face of Jesus stitched on rugged cloth. "I made it myself," she proudly proclaimed. *It's a beautiful piece of art that must have taken her a long time to complete,* I thought, *but what should I do with it? After all, I asked Jesus to restore our marriage and He didn't.* Not wanting to be rude, I accepted the cloth, framed it, and placed it in my bedroom. Today it reminds me that we are never alone.

Walking through Robert Burnaby Park close to our house, I noticed a fallen tree in dense bush. Out of the tree trunk grew five new trees that were strong and soared up to heaven. I stopped to look at this strange configuration and realized that God was giving me a message: "The tree had to be felled to create new life; so be of good cheer." Mahatma Gandhi[8] once said: "A man with a grain of faith in God never loses hope, because he *ever* believes in the ultimate triumph of truth."

BETRAYAL BARRIER

When something goes terribly wrong and the hurt pierces to the very core of our hearts, many believers enter what is called the *betrayal barrier*. The journey begins by examining the purpose of life and exploring if God is real. Little did I know that I was entering this long and dark tunnel myself. It was a journey that took several years to pass through.

I did not realize that this passage was a one-way street with no return. The experience was so powerful that it awakened in me a new spiritual understanding. For lack of a better word, I called this a "rebirth."

During the long and strenuous passage through the tunnel I felt helpless and dependent, but was never alone. Someone was walking with me, watching over me, giving me guidance and encouragement. When I finally stepped out of the abyss on the other side, my family and friends were waiting for me, and welcomed me back with open arms. The world looked friendly again and greeted me with sunshine and warmth. My son Todd encouraged me to play the piano again and I found great enjoyment in doing so. My faith took on a new dimension, a self-realization that there was a God after all. This occurred under a new covenant: I saw a Creator who gives us freedom to choose, permits suffering, and allows us to fall. I also learned that God puts His loving arms around us when we walk in darkness to prevent us from drowning.

Chuck Colson[3], founder of the Prison Fellowship Ministries, says, "Only when we are powerless can we see the strength of God . . . I am convinced that the best things God does are the things that grow out of our weakness and desperation." In 2 Corinthians 12:10 the Apostle Paul writes, "For when I am weak, then I am strong." The nineteenth-century preacher C. H. Spurgeon[17] left us this meaningful reflection:

> We are not strong when we compliment ourselves upon our ability. We are strong when, under a sense of absolute inability, we depend wholly upon God. Only the seed, which the Creator puts into the hand of our weakness, will produce a harvest.
>
> —C.H. Spurgeon

The passage through the betrayal barrier made me bold and fearless. *What is there to lose?* I thought. *Sink or swim!* The time in the gutter helped me become a better person and a stronger leader. Ernest Hemingway[9] writes, "The world breaks everyone, and afterwards, some are strong at the broken places." I like to believe that I became strong at these broken places.

I see the betrayal barrier as *puberty*, a critical passage from childhood to adulthood. As a child we absorb everything that is taught and we believe it. Passing through the teenage years, we begin questioning old rules and challenge the value system. We revolt against authority and seek a new way of life. Only when we grow into adulthood do we regain equilibrium. As puberty forms the bridge from childhood to adulthood, so also does the betrayal barrier provide spiritual maturity, a new underpinning, and a self-realization that there is a God.

Coming out of darkness into daylight, I began to appreciate the little gifts in life. Material things that were important before no longer had the same appeal. An inner joy formed; an awareness of having conquered darkness. I began walking tall above the debris of the broken pieces that lay shattered at my feet. I realized that the very pot I had treasured so much had split open and feared that the crack could never be filled again. Through surrender and acceptance I began understanding that God uses these very cracks to let the light shine in and reveal His great love and glory to us.

Not everyone will find God again after passing through the betrayal barrier, and many will feel abandoned. Dr. R.T. Kendall[11], former senior minister of Westminster Chapel in London, writes that most believers will go through a time when God lets them down. "It is an incorrect view of Scripture to say that we will always comprehend what God is doing and how our suffering and disappointments fit into His plans," he says, and explains further, "Sooner or later, most of us will come to a point when it appears that God has lost control or has lost interest in the affairs of the people. It's only an illusion but one that has dangerous implications for spiritual and mental health."

Dr. Donald Joy[10], a well-known author and speaker, explains that those who rejected faith for cause tend to become more thoughtful believers when they return. They outrank others in commitment and ability to articulate faith. "Who can better speak to agnostics than one who has been there?" Joy exclaims. He hints that the belief in God becomes stronger if the faith is being questioned. Dr. James Dobson[5] expands on this thought by saying, "If the child does not challenge and question what has been taught, then faith remains Mamma's and Daddy's religion instead of his own."

As we get older, we realize that suffering is part of life. Psalm 91:14–16 says, "'Because he loves me,'" says the LORD, "'I will rescue him; will protect him, for he acknowledges my name. He will call upon me, and I will answer him; I will be with him in trouble, I will deliver him and honor him. With long life will I satisfy him and show him my salvation.'"

ACT OF FORGIVENESS

We all get treated unfairly at one time or another. This may be a loss through a theft; an allegation for wrongdoing; a scam causing financial ruin; an injury through someone's careless action; an unfair dismissal at work; stinging remarks made by in-laws and coworkers; or, as in my case, being chastised by a mentally ill spouse. Whatever the circumstances may be, our first response is to lash back. God understands this human trait and teaches us to forgive.

Forgiveness is foreign and unnatural to man. Even if we try to forgive, we are still haunted by the awful wrong that has been done to us. This is especially true if the transgressions are fresh in our minds or are ongoing.

I identify two types of forgiveness and classify them as *mild forgiveness* and *total forgiveness*. Mild forgiveness is an offense that stings when it happens but evaporates with time. Letting go of hurt and forgiving the offender speeds up the healing process. We have no lasting scars, nor are there major disruptions in life, just losses and inconveniences. Total forgiveness, on the other hand, applies to a serious incident that changes our lives for good. The damage does not heal without our making a concerted effort to forgive. If left untreated, the offence will gnaw at our bones and make us bitter and resentful. Let's look at these two forms of forgiveness with examples.

MILD FORGIVENESS

I had the experience of being fleeced by a callous lawyer. After a few preliminary meetings to discuss my divorce, I received a legal bill of CA$6,000, and a requested down payment of CA$30,000 to retain her services. Seeking counsel from another law firm, a retiring lawyer advised me not to pay the bill because it was considered price gouging. This prompted the callous lawyer to summon me to court, and the judge granted a small reduction of the amount I needed to pay.

I was waiting for the adjusted invoice to arrive, but none came. For a while I thought that the lawyer might have forgiven the charge. This was not the case. Three months passed, when the bank informed me that my checks had bounced due to insufficient funds. The bank clerk informed me further that they had received a court order to garnish my funds. It was the lawyer! I remember her saying in one of the chatty meetings, "We lawyers have ways to get the money," and she did it with apparent ease.

Other incidents that fit into the mild forgiveness category were two robberies I experienced while traveling. One involved the theft of my travel bag with passport, personal belongings, and money as part of a trick question at a train station in Düsseldorf, Germany. The other was the theft of my luggage from a hotel lobby in Rio de Janeiro, Brazil. This robbery left me with nothing but the clothes on my back at the beginning of a three-week business trip.

Although upsetting at the time, these transgressions are nothing more than annoyances that don't inflict permanent scars. They sting at first, but we get over them. We learn to become more prudent when hiring a lawyer and traveling abroad. It helps to pass the hurts over to the Lord to let Him look after the aggressors. He will deal with the assailant in a most effective way. Romans 12:19 says: "Do not take revenge, my friends, but leave room for God's wrath, for it is written: 'It is mine to avenge; I will repay,' says the Lord." I was amazed to learn that shortly after the billing incident the lawyer fell ill and abandoned her practice.

As part of writing this book I had the desire to talk to the lawyer again. I located the phone number through an Internet search engine, dialed the number, and was able to reach her in a new town. After exchanging pleasantries, I questioned the billing incident. She remembered my case and said that the litigation was very complex. When I probed her about garnishing my bank account, she sounded surprised at first but then said that this was an acceptable practice. It was good to talk to her. It provided closure.

In-laws and coworkers can also cause frictions that need clemency as part of mild forgiveness. The hurt inflicted often occurs without the party knowing, and forgiveness should be done in private. Uttering into the faces of the offenders, "I have forgiven you for what you've done to me," would be wrong. They might ask, "Forgiven for what? We haven't done anything wrong, have we?" My in-laws may not have realized the sensitive circumstances surrounding the defense of Sophie. They meant well, but the one-sided perception caused a serious misunderstanding between us.

TOTAL FORGIVENESS

In his book *Total Forgiveness,* Dr. R.T. Kendall emphasizes the importance of total forgiveness. "Until you have totally forgiven the other, you will be in chains," he says, and explains that the largest benefit of forgiveness goes to the person who does the forgiving. "You are set free, you are released," Kendall says, and emphasizes that not forgiving and keeping a grudge will hurt the offended person to the point of inflicting physical illness.

Total forgiveness is easier said than done. Take a case in which a partner continually attacks the spouse with threats and verbal abuse, or an assailant who is at large and keeps harassing a helpless victim. This could be aggravation, theft, or rape. How can one forgive if the villain is roaming freely and the victim is in constant fear of further attacks?

The secular model of clemency calls for the removal of the transgressor by putting him behind bars and making him repent while sitting in jail. The authority that passes the sentence believes that correction and healing can only begin in earnest once the blood from the wound has stopped flowing. Cutting into the same wound again and again prevents healing. Although this is helpful and effective, the secular model places all focus on the offender. The authority doing the chastisement is deemed innocent and without sin.

Jesus reminds us that all have sinned and that God also looks at the hearts of those who pass judgment. In the Lord's Prayer we say, "And forgive us our trespasses, as we forgive those who trespass against us." In Mark 11:25 we read: "And when you stand praying, if you hold anything against anyone, forgive him, so that your Father in heaven may forgive you your sins." In Luke 6:27, 32 we read: "Love your enemies, do good to those who hate you, bless those who curse you, pray for those who mistreat you. If you love those who love you, what credit is that to you? Even 'sinners' love those who love them." There is no mention of stopping the transgressor and asking for repentance. Jesus did not request an apology from the mob while He was hanging on the cross. Instead He cried out, "Father, forgive them, for they do not know what they are doing" (Luke 23:34).

Granting total forgiveness demands maturity and a strong spiritual underpinning, prerequisites that are not taught in classrooms, printed in the media, exercised in the business world, or practiced in court. Yet, the very act of total forgiveness is a vital link to regain inner peace and harmony. The late Pope John Paul II did this so well when he offered total forgiveness to Mehmet Ali Agca. Agca shot the Pope while the pontiff was riding in an open car through Saint Peter's Square on May 13, 1981. Two years later the Pope entered Agca's prison cell to offer forgiveness to a man who was a Turkish terrorist. This reflected a Christ-like love toward a most notorious sinner—an act Jesus told us to do.

Dr. Kendall writes further that once we have forgiven we shouldn't tell other people about the hurt endured, not even our closest friends. The incident should come to a closure and be deleted from our mind. But I still catch myself talking about the callous lawyer who emptied my bank account, and mention the wicked thieves who robbed me blind. Does this mean I have not fully forgiven the transgressors? I am certain that I have, even though the experiences are still vivid in my mind.

FORGIVING SOPHIE

Forgiveness was easy during our good times together. This changed when Sophie became uncontrollable and started the frivolous spending spree. Her conniving conduct and blatant disrespect toward me placed a solid wedge between us. I was no longer in the right frame of mind to forgive. Nor could I forgive during the court hearings when we fought tooth and nail over the family assets and business ownership. Sophie's generous divorce settlement, the court-mandated maintenance payments, and her careless squandering of this hard-earned money posed a further hindrance in granting forgiveness.

Today I know that her abrasive behavior and big spending spree were connected to the manic phase of her illness. She no longer has the financial freedom she once enjoyed. The money is long gone and she must depend on my monthly contributions. She has seen me pull through hard times and noted the many bumps and bruises I received along the way. My in-laws now say that she is sorry for what happened and regrets the divorce. By humbling herself, my anger toward her turned to compassion and it became easier for me to forgive.

Would I have been able to forgive had she continued with the insults and disrespect toward me? God knows our stubborn nature and asks us to forgive unconditionally. Forgiving is hard, especially if we have been crushed to the depth of our soul and clemency seems impossible. Credit goes to those who try in spite of the impossible.

Forgiveness does not mean reconciliation, a new friendship, or a restored marriage. Sophie and I will always live separate lives. Nor does forgiveness mean approval of what had been done. The opinions can be miles apart and the parties may never see eye-to-eye. Forgiveness is giving the past over to God, clearing the debris out of the way, and going on with life.

I could not forgive Sophie. Then I began including her in my prayer and a miracle happened! The dark obstacles lifted and my negative thoughts about her evaporated like snow in spring. I saw her as a person again, a human being who has feelings and yearns to be loved and accepted.

If you are unable to forgive, start praying for the aggressor. Total forgiveness may only be possible with prayer because petition removes the chains and sets us free. Being able to forgive brings an eerie feeling of inner joy that has never been experienced before. It is as if God wants to reward us for doing something that seems impossible. The harder the act of forgiveness, the greater the blessing will be. The Lord has a way of measuring the depth of suffering and then returning more than we asked. The person who does the forgiving will be the true victor.

FORGIVING OURSELVES

Realizing the importance of forgiving ourselves, a reader of *Total Forgiveness* asked the author, R.T. Kendall, to teach how to forgive ourselves. Dr. Kendall obliged and wrote the book *How to Forgive Ourselves Totally.*

We all have failed and feel guilty about our misdeeds. Guilt is an emotional state; we know or believe that we have done something wrong. Guilt can be seen as a grieving process that carries on for a season and must eventually be put to rest. Guilt feelings are not bad by themselves. They teach remorse and help us to not want to repeat the wrong. We should not expunge guilt feelings lest we become like Germany's Nazis during World War II. I heard that the Nazi trainees were desensitized by being given a cute little dog to train, and once befriended, were then told to kill the pet in cold blood. This enabled the Nazi to become unscrupulous and carry out the same deeds on humans without feeling guilty.

I identify three types of guilt that need forgiving: *True guilt, false guilt* and *remedial guilt.*

True guilt occurs if someone does something wrong under full knowledge. The responsible person must bring the offense into the open, confess the mistake, accept civil punishment, ask God for forgiveness, and then forgive himself or herself to receive healing. Trying to expunge guilt, as the Nazi killers did, is unnatural and makes forgiveness ineffective. Many former Nazi killers couldn't lead a normal life after World War II and committed suicide.

False guilt is a perceived wrong that arises from a situation that was beyond the person's control. This could be a false judgment or a mishap that came about by unforeseen circumstances. He or she must learn how to unload and move on with life. From my own personal experience, this advice is easier said than done.

My divorce generated intense guilt feelings because I had promised my wife to stay together in sickness and in health. I broke the pledge with full knowledge. The civil court tried me as if I was a convicted criminal, and the penalty was harsh. My friends kept saying that I broke a biblical law and hinted of the consequences. I was reminded again of my heretical status when my church refused entry to an adult-singles dance because I didn't go through an annulment. Then came the accusations by my in-laws, hinting that I had caused Sophie's illness, and they put the blame for the divorce on me. Amassing guilt under these circumstances is normal and forgiving oneself has its challenges.

Remedial guilt is remorse for doing a necessary corrective action. This can be a parent disciplining a child for a wrongful behavior. Even though this deed is necessary as part of good parenting, it often hurts Mom or Dad more than the child when exercised. In a similar way, a manager might grieve when having to reprimand or fire an employee with whom he has had a cordial relationship.

Forgiving oneself is key to deliverance because it sets us free. But even though we have done so, we cannot forget. The emotions linger on, deeply entrenched in our hearts and swelling up again from time to time. Anything can trigger the flashback. This could be a low period in life or reliving a similar experience with someone dear to us.

Difficult times will make us stronger if we are prepared to accept the suffering. Yes, the affliction might have controlled us, and even embittered our hearts for a while. There is a time to let go, and forgiving ourselves will help achieve the freedom we crave for by rising above the darkness that enslaves our soul.

Being conscientious is a fine trait, but over-sensitivity causes nothing but black eyes. We need to put on thicker skin to survive in this rough and rowdy world. We also must learn how to take life easier. It's incorrect to assume that we can escape all problems by simply living a virtuous life. We get sucked up and thrown into the boxing ring even when we stay at a safe distance.

It's always good to add a little humor. Laugh about the things that go wrong and cannot be changed. Learn to joke about falling short of expectations. Proverb 17:22 says: "A merry heart does good, like medicine. But a broken spirit dries the bones" (NKJ). God knows our weakness and understands the emotional scars with which we are struggling. He doesn't want us to wallow in guilt forever, especially if it's not our fault. God is ready to forgive. He wants to lighten our yokes so we can enjoy the gift of life to the fullest.

Forgiveness leads to peace; not forgiving causes evil to triumph. Keeping resentment turns the heart to stone. God wants to give us a heart of flesh because a stony heart cannot give love and will not produce fruit. In Ezekiel 36:26 we read, "I [God] will give you a new heart and put a new spirit in you; I will remove from you your heart of stone and give you a heart of flesh."

The underpinning of forgiveness is *love*. When Jesus said, "Love your enemies, do good to those who hate you, bless those who curse you, pray for those who mistreat you" (Luke 6:27–28), the folks were stunned because such practice was totally new and foreign to them. And yet, expressing love to friend and foe alike is essential in attaining a higher spiritual life. Love raises human dignity and prevents wars. It softens our hearts, strengthens marriages, and forms strong families in which to raise obedient children. Love is the most critical component to a happy and fulfilled life. It surpasses material wealth. Most importantly, however, love provides the ingredient to forgive, one of the key elements to human dignity.

Not everyone is blessed with a healthy mind, and the Bible teaches us to look after the disadvantaged. Supporting a needy "ex" outside marriage fulfills our Christian duty to care for others.

CHAPTER 8

CHRISTIAN DIVORCE

CHRISTIANITY AND DIVORCE

Divorce goes against the grain of every devoted couple. On our wedding day we make a solemn vow before God and our spouse to stay together *through sickness and in health*. A divorce negates the promise and breaks the covenant. However, as my case demonstrates, divorce is sometimes necessary. The untreated mental illness of my wife caused serious dysfunction in my home, which interfered with raising the children. It began with poor school grades and advanced to unlawful conduct outside the home.

I had never imagined that my own children would one day behave in such an unruly and uncontrolled manner. I thought that dysfunctional families and juvenile delinquencies were reserved for a secular lifestyle. In my self-righteous thinking I pointed a finger at this less-than-desirable society. But now, I was plagued with the same problems, and people pointed fingers at me. My hands were tied and I had amazingly little control of the situation. Prayer had no effect. The more I prayed, the worse my situation became—or so it seemed. I dreaded the option of divorce.

PURIFICATION BY FIRE

God allows trials to happen as part of His wise plan. Romans 5:3–4 says: "We rejoice in our sufferings, because we know that suffering produces perseverance; perseverance character; and character hope." Many devout Christians say, however, that a marriage breakup does not qualify for this type of suffering. Our Good Lord would never want us to break a biblical law. Yet, I believe that God includes divorce as part of suffering. The Bible is clear in saying that we must go through all types of trials. Who is to tell us what type of suffering will qualify, and what not? We mature, gain wisdom, and move to the *second phase of life* with a wide range of afflictions.

Franciscan priest, speaker, and author Richard Rohr[15] compares the passing from the first phase to the second phase of life to a baby drinking milk, and then going on to solids when stronger. This "midlife transition," he says, may occur after one has gone through a massive crisis that changed that person's life. This could be a crippling illness, a debilitating accident, the death of a loved one, or a bitter divorce. Rohr explains that God wants to break our egotistical nature—kick us in the butt, so to speak—and when ready, push us into the second phase.

In 1 Peter 1:6–7 we read: "You may for a time have to suffer the distress of many trials; but this is so that your faith, which is more precious than the passing splendor of fire-tried gold, may by its genuineness lead to praise, glory and honor when Jesus Christ appears" (NAB). The fire that the Lord sends does not destroy as a forest fire does, which consumes the trees. Rather, it is like a refiner's fire that purifies by melting down the gold so that the impurities, which interfere with our lives, can be separated. The fire then burns up the contamination and leaves behind the pure gold. It doesn't matter what produces the heat, as long as the intensity reaches the melting point of gold, causes separation, and then engulfs and eliminates the impurities.

Looking back I now realize that my purification process occurred during the betrayal barrier. The gold was heated by fire, liquefied, and the crusty impurities consumed. The liquid metal was then poured into a new mold. In my case, it may have taken a little longer than normal to cool down and become solid again. When I finally surrendered and accepted, 2 Corinthians 12:9 came to mind: "My grace is sufficient for you, for power is made perfect in weakness."

Job, a devout and upright patriarch, was suddenly afflicted by a complete reversal of his fortune. Within a few days all his children died and his wealth vanished. Then a nasty disease ravaged his body and weighed down his soul. Although Job did not understand the suffering, he held onto his faith by saying: "Naked I came from my mother's womb, and naked I will depart. The LORD gave and the LORD has taken away; may the name of the LORD be praised" (Job 1:21).

During Job's time in the gutter, four counselors arrived and insisted that his misfortune was a punishment from God for having done wrong. Job knew better and brushed off their arguments as nonsense. He also ignored his wife, who said to him, "Are you still holding on to your integrity? Curse God, and die." The Bible then goes on to explain that God allowed the devil to test Job. By Job staying steadfast in his faith, the Lord healed him at the end, gave him a new family, and restored his wealth. The teaching of the four counselors proved to be wrong. It was an entrapment of religious legalism bordering on extreme conviction.

In Revelation 3:19 God says, "Those whom I love I rebuke and discipline. So be earnest and repent." These words sound strange from a loving God. It takes great maturity to accept calamity as a God-sent trial, especially when a marriage must be dissolved. Only those who have gone through such a trial will fully understand.

I sometimes wonder if some of us are asked to face more hardship than others. If so, we ask, "Must we suffer to undo the wrongs committed by others as atonement?" We read in Exodus 34:7, "He [God] does not leave the guilty unpunished; He punishes the children and their children for the sin of the fathers to the third and fourth generation." We learn about saints and prophets who bore great misfortune through no fault of their own. Were these people sacrificial lambs who offered atonement so others could have a better life? Let's not forget that Jesus suffered a most agonizing death on the cross to bear our transgressions and grant salvation. Any suffering by humans pales in comparison.

We need to accept afflictions with dignity and endurance. This also applies to divorce. God knows our thoughts and understands our limitations. He only sends what we can endure. The Bible says that the rewards will be great for those who carry the burden to the end. Lamentations 3:31–33 wraps up our thoughts with these words: "For men are not cast off by the Lord forever. Though he brings grief, he will show compassion, so great is his unfailing love. For he does not willingly bring affliction or grief to the children of men."

People with little or no spiritual underpinning may not comprehend suffering and perceive it as unwanted interference that robs life of joy. If a third party is at fault, they hire a lawyer and sue. A rebirth can only begin in earnest if we surrender and accept. God cannot bestow His grace to a person with an angry and unforgiving heart, fists clenched and seeking compensation from court to satisfy a selfish desire. The old debris must first be cleared away and the door to spiritual awareness opened before a divine gift can be given. In the end, the reward received from above will be richer and more enduring than the damage payments mandated by the court.

GOD WORKS IN MYSTERIOUS WAYS

I hadn't yet come to grips with my divorce and was still wrestling with the issue. In my quest for answers, I contacted a high-ranking Catholic Church official in Vancouver to discuss the situation one-on-one. I thought that this saintly reverend might have a better insight into the Lord's mysterious workings than common folks like me.

Catholics are known to have one of the strictest marriage laws, so his explanation caught me by surprise. I had never read what he told me in the Bible. "A civil marriage can and should be dissolved if the spouse causes family problems," the reverend said, and assured me that under the circumstances I had done the right thing. "Divorce is justified if it restores the dignity of the spouse and saves the family," he confirmed, and continued. "No one is obligated to remain in a destructive marriage." He cautioned me, however, that a civil divorce does not pave the way for remarriage; an annulment would be needed.

Relieved but not fully satisfied, I troubled the reverend further by asking, "Why then would God bestow a partner who leads to divorce?" This question caught the church official by surprise and it took him some time to gather his thoughts. He chose his words carefully and began explaining that God gives us freedom to choose. A bad marriage might be sent as a trial similar to an accident or illness to strengthen character, as Romans 5:3–4 says.

While he was speaking, I reached into my briefcase, grabbed the framed family photo that I normally display in my office, and placed it before him. The photo had been taken at the Pan Pacific Convention Center in Vancouver during the entrepreneur award ceremony where I was a finalist. It portrays my daughter in a beautiful red dress and my four handsome sons, all clad in black suits and towering above me in stature.

"Look at what God has done!" I exclaimed.

The church official looked at the family portrait with approval, nodded in agreement and said, "Yes, God works in mysterious ways."

I was probing for answers. More than anything, I was searching for sympathy and approval. Deep inside I felt remorse and wanted to cry on the shoulder of this godly man, pour out my grief, and say, "Look, I prayed and trusted in God, and still the marriage fell apart. Life is not fair. I deserve better." The church official provided an atmosphere of acceptance and healing that helped me accept my fate.

We often dwell on past adversities and don't want to let go. We feed on negativity and blame God for not following *our plan*. The tunnel vision prevented me from seeing how much God had compensated in other ways. Realizing this, I cast down my eyes in awe before the Lord and thanked Him for how much He had done for me. I acknowledged that I was a complainer and asked for understanding and forgiveness.

When tragedy strikes, we begin to realize that our earthly pleasures and possessions can be taken from us at a moment's notice. They are only loaned to us for a short season and when we are asked to let them go, we must abide. There is no such thing as permanency and fairness in this world. The slogan "Life isn't fair" became a common catchphrase in our household and I uttered it whenever my kids complained about perceived unfairness in their young lives.

A good marriage is a gift from God. So is good health. Our bodies are frail, and so are our marriages. When enjoying physical wellbeing, we give credit to our excellent gene pool or a healthy lifestyle that might be attained with a rigorous exercise program or a strict diet. In a good marriage, we pat ourselves on the back for being committed spouses and adhering to biblical principles. We brag that nothing could happen to us and that we have things under control.

Let's not boast, lest we become like the rich man in the Bible. The parable says that everything was going well for him. His labor was rewarded and his fields produced a bountiful harvest. He said to himself, "What shall I do? I have no place to store my crops." Then he said, "This is what I'll do. I will tear down my barns and build bigger ones, and there I will store all my grain and my goods. And I'll say to myself, 'You have plenty of good things laid up for many years. Take life easy; eat, drink, and be merry.' But God said to him, 'You fool! This very night your life will be demanded from you'" (Luke 12:17–20).

Keeping big barns and enjoying the fruit of one's labor is fine, but we are fools to think that a given lifestyle will be ours forever and that it will protect us from the inevitable. Yes, we have some control over good health and a strong marriage, but we cannot change God's plan for us. Divorce was furthest from my thoughts when I married Sophie. And still, it happened.

In his book *Finishing Strong*, author Steve Farrar[7] writes that our ships must be strong to endure the storms of life. He stresses the importance of the *arrival* and not the *journey*. Once we have landed safely, we quickly forget the discomfort of the journey.

What counts at the end is the passing of the baton to the next generation. Strong families, solid companies, and powerful nations find their roots in the founding fathers who overcame diversities through hardship, perseverance, and faith. These leaders humbled themselves before God, asked for guidance, and succeeded in spite of seemingly insurmountable obstacles. Let us remember that:

> It's okay to cry when born. It's okay to cry when we experience disappointments. But if the world cries when we die, then we have finished strong.
>
> —Author unknown

WHOM WE WILL MARRY

Did I make a mistake in marrying my Sophie? Twelve years have transpired since the divorce, and the passing of time has given me deeper insight. Today I asked, "Could God have chosen Sophie to be the mother of my children with full knowledge that the marriage would need to be dissolved after the children were born? Did the Lord deem me as a better father to raise the children than Sophie's former boyfriend with whom she broke up to marry me?" I learned that this man had been unfaithful to the wife he married and divorced. God cares deeply for the welfare of the children, and since Sophie's mental illness could not be prevented, my destiny may have been predestined.

Let's be reminded that we are not placed on this earth for fun and games, but to carry out a God-ordained assignment. Like the biblical prophets who were thrown into many difficult situations, we too are placed in compromising circumstances that we cannot explain.

Life can be compared to a theatrical play in which we become actors performing to a captive audience on stage. In preparation for the play, the director assigns roles for each player. We notice that he gives the most desirable roles to performers who are gifted, attractive, and charismatic. We are second and third in line and must accept less appealing characters. During the play, the audience laughs with delight at the happy scenes and cries with sadness at the tragic moments. When the play is over and the curtain falls, we put on our street clothes and go home, the story still lingering in our minds as we walk through quiet streets. The role we played and the ending that unfolded are now less important than having had the privilege to perform on stage to a captive audience.

In real life we thank God for allowing us to play on the world stage. We are grateful for the freedom bestowed and for the gift of life given, even though our role may be less desirable than envisioned, and the script may be different from what we had wished. We accept the assignment and perform our role to the best of our abilities. God judges us on how we played, and not on the role that had been assigned to us, and the script given.

LIVING WITH DISAPPOINTMENTS

How many of us can say, "My life couldn't be better; everything is going my way; all my dreams are being fulfilled?" I have not met one person who could say so. We all live with disappointments. In spite of this,

God gives us moments of joy that are so beautiful and powerful, they compensate for the less pleasant times and make life worth living.

In the following word-pictures we look at human desires that were short-lived but brought happiness and enlightenment in spite of their brevity.

A couple married in good faith, enjoyed a happy family life, but divorced because of unforeseen difficulties. If we were to ask them today, "Would it have been better if you had not married?," they would likely reply, "No, getting married and starting a family was good. We shared many happy times and the intimate moments provided love and fulfillment. Being married offered unforgettable moments that we couldn't have enjoyed otherwise."

In another word-picture a couple is happily married and has one child. They prayed earnestly to have a second one, but instead of their wish being fulfilled, the child falls ill and dies before reaching school age. Asking the parents, "Would it have been better had the child never been born?," they would say, "We're thankful for having had her, even though the time was short." The love given and the affection returned are eternal, an experience that cannot be taken away, even in death. The child lives on in memory, always young, energetic, and loving.

Our life is built on memories. Memory is a virtual photo album that we treasure throughout our life. I remember the snowmen I built with my brothers while growing up on the farm. Of course they have long melted away, but the joy of having made them continues to live on. These memories return to us when we help our own children erect snowmen again.

We see beautiful sand castles being sculpted on beaches. Talented artists create these pieces of art with the full knowledge that the incoming tide will wash them away. The nostalgia and friendship of building them lives on even though they existed for only a day. In a similar way, God sees our earthly accomplishments as nothing more than melting snowmen and washed-up sand castles. I am certain that the Lord takes great delight in seeing our handiwork and shares in the enthusiasm, even though they are here today and gone tomorrow.

We expect our gifts to last a lifetime. A marriage should endure until death; children should outlive their parents and help them in their old age. We are quick to blame God if things go wrong because we have ordered a long-term relationship. As devoted Christians, we expect exclusive privileges—a first-class ticket to fulfillment.

Let us be reminded that prayer and devotion do not guarantee a trouble-free life. Such expectations would be a wrong view of Christian faith. We must accept the plan that God has laid out for us, even if it strays from the desired path. God does not pledge satisfaction on earth, nor does He give us special rights. On the contrary: the Lord might assign us a role that is extremely difficult to play on the theatrical stage. He chooses us because we are best suited for the task. Good looks and charisma, attributes that are so important in this world, are less significant to God. These physical qualities could become a hindrance rather than an asset. Musician and singer Louis Armstrong had a gravelly voice but his singing was beautiful, musical, and sincere. Beauty does not come from perfection but spills forth from the heart.

Jesus understood human suffering under the bondage of rigid rules and offered compassion, proclaiming: "Peace I leave with you; my peace I give you. I do not give to you as the world gives. Do not let your hearts be troubled and do not be afraid" (John 14:27). Faith, surrender, and acceptance provide this inner peace.

CHAPTER 9

MENTAL ILLNESS IN MARRIAGE

ALTERED LEVEL OF CONSCIOUSNESS

Folks are at a loss in what to do when visiting a mentally ill person. They see the frustration that the healthy spouse experiences in caring for a sick partner and realize how little they can do to help. In many ways, mental infirmity is more devastating than a physical illness because an unsound mind robs a person of the ability to think clearly.

Uncertain what to expect, many acquaintances hesitate to call on a mentally ill patient. This, however, shouldn't be an excuse to stay home. When visiting, the caller should remember three basic rules: First, a psychiatric disorder does not heal like a physical wound. Second, the patient may be in denial and does not admit having an affliction. But the most important third rule is understanding that the ill person is a human being who seeks love and acceptance in a world that has become estranged.

The visitor may find the patient behaving absolutely normal. He or she is jovial, optimistic, and wants to conquer the world. This ecstasy may only be a fragile veneer that can easily be broken with a careless remark. At another call, the ill person may be cold and aloof. Comforting doesn't help, and rather than accepting empathy, the patient may blame the visitors, thinking they are the villains who have come to bring anguish. He or she may utter inappropriate remarks, putting the guests on the spot and making them uncomfortable. And then, there are times when the patient is so depressed that he or she doesn't want to socialize. The caller must accept the condition of the day and exercise patience. Lending a listening ear is always the best contribution one can make.

When Sophie was living on her own after the divorce, Frank and Mary paid a visit to the apartment she managed by herself. They expected to be welcomed cordially, as they had always been when visiting our home in Burnaby. But instead of being received with the customary smile, Sophie made slanderous remarks. In her confused mind, she thought the friends had come to plot against her and cause physical harm. Luckily, her condition has since improved and she enjoys a close circle of friends again.

Not all folks with mental illness are paranoid. Many do well living in a caring community. Accepting the illness and taking the prescribed medication is key to achieving stability. Equally, if not more important, is the human touch. Dr. Frank Ayd (1920–2008), a psychiatrist who studied early antipsychotic and the use of antidepressant drugs said, "Medication is no substitute for compassion, nor does it replace patience and lending an attentive ear." Hearing these words from the architect of antidepressant drugs is refreshing in a world that relies so heavily on pharmaceutical products.

The Christian community strongly disapproves of divorce. One hears of moving testimonials of couples who have stayed married in spite of debilitating illnesses, such as paralysis, blindness, brain injury, cancer, and Parkinson's and Alzheimer's diseases. They want to keep the family together at all cost, even if it means caring for the spouse 24 hours a day. They say that divorce is never an option, and believe that God will give them the grace and strength to make a seemingly insurmountable task possible.

When the movie *A Beautiful Mind* opened in December 2001, the mental health community called it a winner. It tells a story of a Nobel Prize-winning mathematician who suffered from schizophrenia. He eventually overcame the disability and returned to his career as a brilliant university professor. The tireless support of his wife drew applause from families in similar situations. Alicia, who loved and always believed in her husband, took on the role as breadwinner, monitored his medication, and refused to give up even when his prognosis looked hopeless. Such a turnaround would not have been possible had she dumped him.

As we applaud Alicia as the real hero of the story, we secretly question whether we could do the same, especially with children involved. Watching someone else's story unfold on screen hardly touches the day-to-day frustrations, tears, and fears of actually living the saga. I should mention that Hollywood got creative and added some coloration for the sake of the box office.

The *HealthyPlace.com* article "A member of your family is Mentally Ill—What Now?" addresses the unique needs of those living with someone who battles schizophrenia, bipolar disorder, depression, or any other serious mental illness. "The strains of mental illness on a marriage may be devastating. 'There is a very high divorce rate among people who have depression or bipolar disorder,' says Nassir Ghaemi, [a Harvard professor interviewed in the article]."[a]

I found living with a mentally ill spouse unworkable. Having been her punching bag for so many years, being disrespected and blamed for everything, I eventually reached the end of my rope and could no longer cope. Advisors suggest giving more attention to the ill spouse, but this didn't work for me. On the contrary, it only exacerbated the problem, and I had to distance myself from her on purpose. It is common that the ill person is most difficult to those who are very close to them and provide the most care. I respect anyone who is trying to keep a marriage together against all odds and congratulate them if they succeed. God understands our limits.

Friends Who Help or Hinder

Throughout our family crisis I kept in touch with my good friends and asked them for guidance. Being a practicing Christian, I gravitated toward folks with a conservative view. I perceived them as the wiser bunch with the right answers. However, when my problems continued and they kept insisting that divorce was wrong, I changed my mind and went my own way. Keeping a dysfunctional marriage alive for the sake of religious rules began troubling me. As we began diverting further in our thinking, I started to realize that people who never had to endure deep hardship could not effectively guide those traveling on a difficult road. They assume, "For whatever a man sows, that he will also reap" (Gal. 6:7).

"Tell the Lord what you need and He will answer your prayer," they encouraged me. "Join our church and God will melt away your problems. The Bible promises so." At first, I took these supportive words to heart and let my hopes rise, only to be crushed again, worse than before.

"You are not praying right," my Christian friend objected. "Or perhaps you have disobeyed God's commands. The Lord will help." After a while, these comments began to annoy me. *What experience do these folks have in advising me on marriage and divorce when they've never had to crash-land a plane with engines on fire,* I thought. I began brushing off their advice as goodwill gestures and kept looking for more practical answers.

Blaise Pascal[14] (1623–1662), the great French philosopher and mathematician, once said that there are only two types of people in the world: The *seekers* and the *non-seekers*. I am a *seeker*, and being at a crossroad I could no longer accept textbook answers as the be-all and end-all solutions to life. I searched for a deeper meaning—a way of life that lay outside the well-traveled path of the ordinary.

My friends noticed my change and tried to prop up my falling faith by quoting Romans 8:28: "And we know that in all things God works for the good of those who love him, who have been called according to his purpose." Although well intentioned, this was the worst possible time to recite this verse. The words crashed down upon me like a ton of bricks. "God working for the good of those who love him?" I wanted to scream. "What possible good does a mental illness have that tears a family apart? Who in the world would put such a text in the Bible? Unrealistic and nonsense at best!"

Bible verses do help people in trouble, but let me advise the reader to go easy on them. Quoting scriptural verses when someone's mind is in a knot can be perceived as preaching from the hilltops. Instead, lift up the troubled person by sympathizing with them and giving hope. Find examples of other families that have made it through the crisis.

Most importantly, give love and support by being there and allowing the person to express his or her feelings. By doing so, you put biblical teaching to work rather than preaching it.

A divorce is one of the most difficult trials a human faces. The helping friend must be strong, practical, and not be overcome by emotion. He or she must *respond* rather than *react* to the situation. When divorce draws closer, you, as the mediator, should guide the person to the next step. This may include finding a good lawyer and a new place to live. It might also mean talking to the children and explaining to them that these steps are necessary. A confirming voice from a mature adult outside the home will moderate their fears. This is especially important when they see their beloved mom or dad leave or being taken away by the authorities, forever altering their lives. You become the anchor in whom the children will find refuge at a time when their own parent might be overburdened with legal and social issues.

Until now we have only addressed the custodial parent and the care of the children. Let's not forget the non-custodial parent who is alone and also needs love and attention. Who can offer the much-needed help for the estranged partner, especially if he or she is ill? It's not fair that a dear family member is being tossed out of the home and forgotten because he or she no longer fits into the home. The Bible says we must take care of the sick and needy. The very person who might be in greatest need is often overlooked.

We must set priorities, and as harsh this may sound to some, I rank the family members highest. The welfare of the children must come first to put them at ease. Number two is making certain that the custodial parent has the physical and mental stability to cope with the changes. Only then can we meet the need of the disposed parent.

Some may stand up and shout "unfair"—and they are right. But let those who raise their voices the loudest be the first to help. It's biblical to do so. Fortunately, Sophie's sister and husband were kind enough to take her in and care for her. They did an excellent job, and I would like to thank them for this. If in-laws and friends cannot assist, government authorities have the responsibility to assist.

I had the support of Frank and Mary and I am truly thankful for their help, even though they didn't agree with the divorce and were a bit heavy on Bible verses. Romans 8:28 didn't work for me then. My circumstances were out of sync with something "working for the good." I have a better understanding now and see the picture in a broader view. Although we had our disagreements during the critical moments, we are best friends again and enjoy one another's company.

The Bible offers many excellent verses that will help a troubled heart. Reciting one or two to a hurting person might entice him or her to open the Bible and read on. The book of Psalms is particularly calming. Here are some of my favorite verses that are good to share:

- Be strong and courageous. Do not be afraid or terrified . . . for the LORD your God goes with you; He will never leave you nor forsake you (Deut. 31:6).
- So do not fear, for I am with you; do not be dismayed, for I am your God. I will strengthen you and help you; I will uphold you with my righteous right hand (Isa. 41:10).
- The righteous cry out, and the LORD hears them; he delivers them from all their troubles. The LORD is close to the brokenhearted and saves those who are crushed in spirit. A righteous man may have many troubles, but the LORD delivers him from them all (Ps. 34:17–19).
- The LORD is near to all who call on him . . . He fulfills the desires of those who fear him; He hears their cry and saves them (Ps. 145:18–19).
- Trust in the LORD with all your heart and lean not on your own understanding; in all your ways acknowledge Him, and He will make your paths straight (Prov. 3:5–6).
- Come to me, all you who are weary and burdened, and I will give you rest. Take my yoke upon you and learn from me, for I am gentle and humble in heart, and you will find rest for your souls (Matt. 11:28–29).

SOLID ANSWER ON DIVORCE

In this concluding paragraph of Part Two, we address divorce and the Bible. This is a delicate topic, and I confess that I am not qualified to discuss this with great accuracy. I am not a Bible expert. I have read the

Bible several times cover-to-cover, and my perception is that of a layman. But then . . . most of us are laymen and have a limited understanding. When we discuss divorce and the Bible, we talk layman-to-layman.

Divorces will continue to happen; some are necessary, but most are preventable. Many couples get a divorce when they shouldn't; others stay married when a divorce would be better. A divorce should never occur if the partners are blessed with a healthy and rational mind. As much as we desire this dignified state, the human brain often fails, and so does the relationship. If this occurs, a divorce is often the only alternative to keep one's own sanity and prevent the family from falling apart. Verse 2383 of the Catholic Catechism[2] says this about a marriage that needs resolving:

> If civil divorce remains the only possible way of ensuring certain legal rights, the care of the children, or the protection of inheritance, it can be tolerated and does not constitute a moral offense.
>
> —Catholic Catechism, Verse 2383

Second Chronicles 1:10 says: "Learn to be wise and develop good judgment and common sense." I took this Bible verse to heart and came up with my own directive as to when a couple should step out of a troubled marriage. The aim is to liberate the disadvantaged spouse from an unworkable marriage by restoring human dignity and building a functional home in which to raise obedient children. Having said this, allow me to say that:

1. *Divorce is recommended* if the behavioral disorder of one spouse destroys the dignity of the other, endangers family assets, causes medical problems, and the situation cannot be reversed.
2. *Divorce is necessary* if the behavior of the spouse causes the family to become dysfunctional, interferes with raising the children, and such behavior cannot be reversed.
3. *Divorce is necessary* if the partner endangers the personal safety of the spouse and/or the children, and the condition is continuing with no sign of change.

I admit that I have gone beyond biblical interpretations and ask you to use your own discretion. The reason for my deviation is simple: I have a hard time understanding the biblical reasoning behind divorce. The Mosaic law of the Old Testament made it too easy for a man to divorce his wife. Simply issuing a certificate of divorce for any fickle reason could put her away. The New Testament added new rules that permit divorce if: (1) the marriage occurred prior to salvation, (2) the mate is guilty of sexual immorality, and (3) the mate is an unbeliever and deserts the believing partner.

These New Testament rules are the more accepted guidelines in Christian circles, but they don't fit well into today's culture, as far as I can tell. For one, the demeanors are correctable. The couple has the choice to adjust, change the way of life, and make the marriage work. Behavior problems and mental illness, on the other hand, are permanent and continue with their destructive path.

We must appreciate that the New Testament was written when Christianity was young and needed protection similar to a tree sapling planted in fresh soil. The biblical writers wrote what lay on their hearts and what was most important at that time. Marriage laws, as we know them today, did not exist then.

I am so bold as to say that I cannot find workable answers in the Bible on divorce, nor are all church ministers supportive. "Our hands are bound by the Bible," many said when I ask specific questions. This ambiguity concerns me, especially in light of today's high divorce rate. Without solid answers from church leaders, the affected person has no other option than to seek answers from secular sources. In the secular world, the hands are not bound.

Many thinking Christians struggle with the Bible. This is a serious issue that is being ignored by many church leaders and must be addressed more openly. Allow me to assure the reader that I am not in disagreement with the Bible. The many scriptural references quoted in this book ensure my full support of Scripture. I am concerned, however, with the *rigid interpretation* of the words of the Bible. This can be obstructive to those facing a serious crisis. Isolating verses from the Bible while ignoring the greater biblical exhortation that include compassion, peace, and freedom can have serious implications. Narrowing one's mind to a tunnel vision does not fare well in our modern culture. We must unbind rather than bind our hands, and Jesus did this so effectively when He lived among us.

Are we able to turn to the Bible for definitive answers on such important issues as marriage and divorce? I believe that in finding biblical truth we must look beyond isolated texts and search for the deeper meaning, bearing in mind the totality of the biblical message and the cultural influences, which shaped the biblical text on such topics as marriage and divorce. We must be prepared to explore current day problems in light of biblical principles rather that applying unbending rules on passages that are taken out of context. There may come a time when one cannot live by strict biblical interpretations alone, and I strongly believe that an irresolvable behavior problem can and should be a valid reason for divorce.

Pastors who provided critical support in writing this book also expressed concern that the Bible is unclear on *divorce for just cause* and wished better guidelines were given. A Catholic priest said that the church has never held the position that we are obligated to remain in a destructive marriage. He suggested that separation may be required if medical and psychological treatments are unsuccessful. In his view, continuing with such a relationship would simply be unbearable, and a civil divorce might be necessary for financial reasons to stop a money leak. The priest elaborated further that governments provide many services today to help mentally challenged people survive outside of marriage. These amenities were not available during biblical times, and a person was fully dependent on the spouse for support.

Times and cultures have changed and I believe that the responsible parent is the most qualified judge in deciding what's best for the family. A mother and father carry the ultimate responsibility in raising the children. Yes, marriage is meant to be permanent, but nowhere does the Bible say that we must stay in a dysfunctional marriage.

Jesus asked the crowd, "If any of you has a sheep and it falls into a pit on the Sabbath, will you not take hold of it and lift it out? How much more valuable is a man than a sheep!" (Matt. 12:11–12). Sabbath was (and still is) a day of rest and Jesus performed many miracles on that day. He did this to demonstrate that there is no law against doing good on a Sabbath. He wanted to show to the Pharisees that a loving relationship with God and neighbor takes precedence over laws that keep people enslaved by fear and hopelessness.

How I wished we could ask Jesus again on such sensitive issues as *divorce for just cause*. He liberated himself from rigid rules and took the common-sense approach. He received his people with unconditional love and always placed compassion ahead of observance of man-made laws. He grabbed the lamp stand and placed it where light was needed.

Some religious leaders have taken the same lamp stand and anchored it in concrete. If the light does not shine where illumination is needed, then we are out of luck. Rigid Bible interpretation can inhibit rather than enlighten God's enduring message to us. The lamp becomes a stationary object that is biblically correct but only satisfies the authority that delivers the interpretation. Applied in a dictatorial way, the religious laws become a rod that smites, and the Bible becomes a religious entrapment rather than liberation. No one wants to go back and be ruled by the Pharisees of old. Religious extremism has kept many devout Christians from entering a church again.

Rules are necessary and we must obey them. However, rules can only work if they benefit citizens, parents, and children. There is a time when one must look beyond rigid textbook laws and use our God-given intellect. The path we choose may not always agree with established conventions. God supports our choices and blesses them if done in love and good faith.

The good news is that we are never alone when the going gets tough. God will send helpers when chosen organizations fail. This assistance came to me numerous times without fail—it arrived from the hands of ordinary laymen. "'For this is what the Sovereign LORD says: I myself will search for my sheep and look after them. As a shepherd looks after his scattered flock when he is with them, so will I look after my sheep. I will rescue them from all the places where they were scattered on a day of clouds and darkness'" (Ezek. 34:11–12).

We pray that our churches will be a gathering place where God rescues the lost sheep and guides them to the light—a place where everyone will find a home, whether married, divorced, or single, for we all have sinned and need God's mercy and forgiveness.

PART III
DOING IT ALONE

Photo by Michael A. Wollen, www.mindtapmedia.com

CHAPTER 10

RAISING A FAMILY AS A SINGLE PARENT

I n these concluding chapters we leave the reasoning on divorce behind and focus our discussion on rebuilding the family and rearing the children. The reckoning is over. There is nothing more we can do other than to accept and submit. Rather than searching for justifications and wallowing in guilt, crying out, *Life isn't fair*, we grab the bull by the horns and march steadfast into the future, fulfilling our obligation as the sole leader of the family. The wounds from the divorce may still hurt, but the theatrical play must go on because we have a household of hungry kids to feed. We pack our emotions into boxes, seal them tight, and place them in the attic. With the obstacles removed and out of the way, we begin building a new home by doing everything possible to bring joy and happiness into the family. The children will remember these efforts for the rest of their lives and thank us for the labor.

DOING DOUBLE DUTY

God gave the obligation of raising children to two parents, a mother and a father. At least this was His original plan. As much as we would like to adhere to this powerful model, the desire of a two-parent family is not always attainable, even with the best intentions. Before we know it we find ourselves raising the family alone. Dr. James Dobson[5] from Focus on the Family says, "Being a single parent is the most difficult job on earth."

A parent must obey many masters, each shouting for attention. One of these masters is *money*. Financial liquidity is especially critical if the parent is also the sole breadwinner. The expenses of running a household are staggering and there is often little cash left to tie the family over to the next payday. Frugal money management and staying out of debt cannot be emphasized enough.

In learning how to serve the many masters of a household, a parent must create a delicate balance of work, housekeeping chores, family time, and rest. Most importantly, we must find a way to conserve energy and avoid burnout. Since we only have 16 hours of productive time a day and cannot add more, even if we wanted to, we may need to set our expectations a notch below the accepted norm. A single parent cannot devote the same attention to detail as a two-parent family could. It's all right if the house is a bit messier than that of the neighbors, or if there are fewer outdoor activities, as long as the home is filled with sincerity and love.

Allow me to share a few family models that worked well for us. Your household may be different and your parenting skills better than mine, so pick the examples that best apply to your home. I am not speaking as a professional with a degree, but as a father who learned on the job by trial and error.

Nanny-Housekeeper

Working parents with small children often resort to a nanny-housekeeper for babysitting and general housekeeping duties. This worked well for us when the children were small. I enjoyed coming home to a clean house, cooked meals, and ironed shirts. But too much help around youngsters can have a negative effect, especially when the children get older. Once my youngest turned fourteen I let the nanny go. This is the time when the kids were old enough to look after their own affairs, such as housecleaning and doing laundry. With a nanny in waiting, the youngsters dropped their dirty socks and underwear wherever they pleased and expected them to be washed, folded, and back in the drawer the next day. Having to look after their clothes alleviated these problems.

A nanny can also cause havoc with eating habits. Our Filipina nanny cooked the meals in the afternoon and the children indulged themselves when they came home from school. Then at suppertime, no one was hungry and I ate the reheated food by myself. With the nanny gone I started preparing the meals and we began eating together as a family again.

Quality Time

Children remember ordinary times best when family members participated and have fun. Just working in the vegetable garden gave little Todd so much enjoyment that he said, "Dad, this is the *bestest* time I've ever had." We always made Christmas and birthdays a special occasion to celebrate. Our photo albums are filled with happy moments of opening gifts, singing Happy Birthday, and blowing out candles on the birthday cake.

Every family has their own customs, and ours was cutting apples into "apple-boats" and pears into "pear-wheels." There I was, standing at the kitchen counter with knife in hand, cutting apple-boats and pear-wheels until everyone was satisfied. These fruits served as desert after a meal or snack before going to bed. Such family activity promotes time together and entices the children to eat more fruit.

One of the high-points of the day was tucking the children into bed. Like all kids, mine disliked going to bed, but with bedtime stories this event became more enjoyable. I allowed two stories each. Request for the third and sometimes the fourth were pure delaying tactics. I would read from a children's Bible or the five-volume storybook we had purchased. Some episodes were so heroic and moving that my voice would choke while reading them. We always said a short prayer before turning off the light.

School Activities

Parents are asked to participate in many school activities, such as organized sports. As a single parent, I was careful as to how much time I could afford. I went to a few events but seldom stayed long. I missed being there when my youngsters did well. Seeing a child excel fills a parent's heart with inner joy and satisfaction, and all my children did well in sports.

Counselors and authors say that nothing is more important than being there for your children, supporting them in their activities, and encouraging them to excel. I strongly agree with this, but I took exception. My business was depriving me of many hours that other parents could spend freely outside the home. My work was necessary; it provided a vital support to press through many financial rough spots that came along.

Today, my children are proud and thank me that I was able to do both jobs: running a business and raising the family. They understood my multitasked obligations and allowed me to pursue what I thought was best. Mature children do not insist on taking up too much of the parent's time. They know that Mom and Dad have other responsibilities. Our affluent society has conditioned children to demand too much from the parents. Kids call for *room service* at any fickle moment and the parent runs. This was not the case with large rural families in the past, nor can parents afford this type of service in poorer countries. It's a sign of the developed Western society. I encourage moms and dads to participate in their children's activities, but let no one pressure you into how you should devote your time. Each family situation is different. Just try to do your best.

Chauffeur Duties

Driving the children to school and other scheduled events takes a big chunk out of a parent's time, and few single parents can afford to do much of this. The home should be located in a convenient location with amenities in walking distance. This gives the children the freedom to roam around without asking the parent to drive all the time.

We were fortunate to live in a neighborhood where the youngsters could walk to school, the dentist, the doctor, and the stores. Destinations farther away were accessible by bus. I simply wasn't able to be a "soccer dad" and drive the kids to sports events, ballet instructions, and piano lessons. They might have done better in piano had I chosen a better teacher, but I was prepared to make this compromise. Something has to give when raising a family alone.

If your children walk to school, emphasize safety when crossing busy roads. Many parents are also worried about child abductions and child abuse. These are unfortunate developments in our times that rob children of their God-given freedom to move around freely. Teaming up with other children will make the walk to and from school safer and more enjoyable. Such a group effort, however, is only possible if the neighborhood children are also asked to walk. Being outdoors and walking provides a great health benefit, not to mention reducing traffic gridlock, lowering greenhouse gases, and conserving energy.

Parents' Actions and Words

Children observe their parents' actions without them knowing. Deeds speak louder than words. Youngsters also remember the parent's goof-ups and how they dealt with them. Children with a strong and silent father who speaks little but acts on what he says do better than those with a talkative dad who always preaches but doesn't follow his own rules. It is also known that the older we get, the more we pursue the steps of our parents, even though we may not always have liked what they did. I had many run-ins with my dad, but I appreciated his solid lifestyle. I am now becoming more and more like him.

Church Attendance

Going to church has a positive effect on the family. It sets the foundation of future religious activities of the children as they look up to their parents, especially the father, for moral and spiritual guidance. Even if the youngster has a good excuse not to go, knowing that mom and/or dad attends is most beneficial.

The results of a study in Switzerland reveals that the leadership of a father, and to a lesser extent the mother, in attending church forms an important directive for future religious thinking in the children. With the head of the family attending regular church services and the mother non-practicing, 44 percent of the children became churchgoers. If, on the other hand, the mother attends regularly and the father is non-practicing, only two percent of their children became frequent church attendees. The study does not explain the reason for the difference, but emphasizes that church-going mothers also have a very positive influence to the family; it prevents the children from drifting away entirely.[a]

During teenage years, church attendance frequently drops off and God is placed on the back burner. Getting married and having children of their own revives spiritual interest. The young couple will remember their own upbringing and develop a desire to follow in the footsteps of their parents. It's important that at least one family member keep the conduit to God's blessings open by going to church. Daily prayer is also important. At ninety, my mother's prayer acts like a well of fresh water that trickles down and nourishes the root system of our family tree.

Perception of Fairness

Children want fairness and look for law and order. One always hears kids say, "This isn't fair," and my family was no exception in such utterance. Fairness is at the root of a solid family structure, and I believe that God gave the authority of law and order to the father. The mother, on the other hand, is better in fostering the emotional needs of the children. As we require justice and love, we can see that we need both parents in raising a balanced and well-adjusted family. If this is not possible, young children do better with the mother and the older children with the father.

SHARING MEALS TOGETHER

Eating meals as a family forms a strong bond because food serves as a common ambition that ties family members together. After a meal we share the satisfaction of a full tummy and the companionship of having done it together.

With five hungry youngsters, the food consumption at the Buchmann household was huge. I literally hauled in groceries by the truckload (minivan). One grocery cart was hardly large enough to carry the load, and I would hang extra bags off both sides of the cart. Bystanders at the checkout counter would ask, "Are you running a cruise ship?," to which

I'd say, "Almost!" Our household was jokingly dubbed "the house of food" because my boys liked to invite their friends to eat with us.

A national survey conducted by the National Center on Addiction and Substance Abuse at Columbia University found that children who regularly eat with their families have fewer behavioral problems in school than families that eat on the fly. They are also less likely to take illicit drugs, drink alcohol, and get involved in premarital sex.[b]

The 2003 CASA (National Center on Addiction and Substance Abuse at Columbia University) survey of adults and teens found that teens who ate dinner five to seven times a week with their families were 21 percent less likely to try tobacco or alcohol; 17 percent less likely to try marijuana; and eight percent more likely to get A's in school than those who seldom or never shared family meals. The survey concluded that teenagers who have dinner with their families only two nights a week or less are at double the risk of substance abuse than teens who share more frequent family dinners. Furthermore, researchers at the University of Minnesota reported that teens who ate seven or more meals with their families each week had higher grade-point averages, were less likely to feel depressed, consume alcohol, smoke cigarettes, or use marijuana than those who ate with their families less than twice a week. Numerous other studies have also demonstrated the benefit of eating family meals together.

The family dinner is an endangered tradition in many households, and the 2003 University of Minnesota study involving nearly 300 families discovered that a third of the participants felt their family was too busy to eat dinner as a group. No matter how simple the meal or how pressed for time we are, parents should make the effort to sit down and enjoy meals together as a family. Why not make this a pleasant experience and enjoy quality time? Leave the arguments and disciplining for later. Time spent breaking bread with family and friends will not only help our children form positive attitudes about food and eating habits, it will also create fond memories about togetherness that lasts a lifetime.

Family and food belong together. How many grown-ups still say, "No one can prepare a meal as well as Mom!" It may not have been the food that was so delicious but the thought of a caring mother preparing it especially for us. It was an act of love that filled our tummy. It made us feel good, and we became big and strong. Food has tied families together since time immemorial.

RELATIONSHIPS

Parents want a good relationship with the children, but this noble desire becomes a challenge during the teenage years. The awful things youngsters say during adolescence are often a test to see if we really are who we say we are. As parents we try keeping cool, but heated outbreaks happen anyway. This mostly occurs at awkward moments when everyone's patience is stretched to the limit. Parents and kids say unkind words, and the situation easily gets out of hand.

When the crisis is over we wonder what on earth has brought on such a commotion and we blame ourselves for not having handled the situation better. We fret about how emotional we can get over seemingly insignificant events if provoked at the wrong time.

After tempers subside, both parties should offer apologies for their irrational behavior and inappropriate words spoken. By admitting one's shortcomings the youngster will realize that a parent is also vulnerable and makes mistakes. As both parties mop up, the parent and youngster should be drawn closer together. The calm after the storm provides quality moments to open up, share feelings, and try understanding each other better.

Apologies and a blissful calm after the squall are not always the norm and all too often the parties remain divided. Unresolved business eventually causes a division between a parent and a child. This leads to hostility. If allowed to continue, the youngster becomes distant from the parent and goes his or her own way. Anger and resentment set in and the relationship begins to suffer.

This happened with my father and me. After an argument, my dad would simply ignore me and I was not in the mood to sort things out. As time went on we had many unresolved issues that made me distant from him. I also have disagreements with my teenagers and we don't always resolve the issues amicably. The loggerhead syndrome of the Buchmann family is being passed down to the next generation.

The proverb, "Children should be seen and not heard" may no longer apply in modern families. In his weekly column, Dr. Charles Cummins[4] asks his readers, "Were you allowed to participate in adult conversations when you were young?" Those encouraged to speak did better socially in life than those who had to remain silent. A child who is accepted by the adult world builds self-confidence at an early age. A good father-son relationship is especially important. Perhaps this assurance was missing when I grew up because our European culture taught us to remain silent with visitors. One generation later my young children spoke freely, participated in discussions with our friends, and told their own stories, even though they didn't always understand the topic talked about.

VISITING HOURS

Allowing an "ex" to visit the family home is awkward no matter what arrangements have been made. This is especially true if the wounds of the divorce are still fresh and the behavioral quirks that led to the divorce continue. Visiting hours are arranged mostly outside the parental home, but the court made an exception for us. The children were still young and couldn't travel by bus to Langley to visit their mother.

Sophie's visiting hours were scheduled for Saturdays at my house. She was an early riser and arrived way too soon for my liking. Her knock on the door interfered with the unhurried breakfast that I enjoyed on weekends. To avoid surprises I tried to get out of the house before she arrived. She also visited during the week and her unscheduled appearances began bothering me. The children understood my desire for autonomy and alerted me to her presence when I came home from work.

Sophie expressed her love to the children in many ways. She was a nurturing mother who brought many gifts, took them shopping, and ate at restaurants. They liked her generous manner, unhurried disposition, and just spending time together. In comparison, I was the disciplinarian who prepared home-cooked meals and had little spare time, or patience, or money for extracurricular activities.

Was there competition in getting the children's favor? You bet there was. I worked hard to keep up my popularity. There's bound to be friction when one parent does the hardcore duties of running a household while the other comes for friendly visits with bags full of gifts and goodies. Each of us wanted to instill in the children what we thought was best, but our perceived values diverged. Sophie's emphasis was on meeting their very material needs and desires. I, on the other hand, worried about spoiling them rotten by giving too much. Lack of communication in custody disputes causes serious misunderstandings that can lead to mistrust and tension.

In spite of the perceived interference and apparent indulgence, Sophie's visits had a positive spin on the children. The boys needed the tenderness of their mother. Her presence offered a balance to the otherwise male-dominated boot camp that ran like the Swiss Army.

Her visits also taught the children how to care for their mother. The youngest two looked after her especially well. At first they didn't notice much wrong with Mom and wanted her to stay at home for good. They didn't understand why she couldn't move back in, and were saddened that she had to leave again in the evening.

The children loved their mother and had forgotten about the less pleasant times of the past. Todd could not remember the incident as a preschooler when he asked me to send Mom away so we could have a happy Christmas. God wires the brains of children to unload unpleasant events that could interfere with the journey in life.

CHAPTER 11

RESPONSIBILITY OF
A PARENT

WHEN DIVORCE IS A SOLUTION

Why do some youngsters do well while others go astray, although the home setting may be similar? I cannot solve this puzzle other than by sharing my own experience in raising a family under disadvantaged circumstances. Let me remind the readers again that I am not writing as an expert with professional degrees, but as a father who has observed the rise and fall of his family.

There is evidence that children from broken families experience greater problems in school, get poorer grades, are more tempted to break the law, and have bigger health issues than those from well-functioning two-parent families. Blaming the problems on single parenthood is an oversimplification that may lead to a wrong conclusion. Instead of pointing the finger at divorce, we must go deeper and examine what caused the family breakup in the first place. We do this by evaluating the character of the couple.

A marriage can only succeed if both partners are rational and mature. Self-sacrifice and servanthood, two ingredients that are vital in a good marriage, are often missing in a troubled marriage. These shortcomings interfere with forming a stable family in which to raise obedient children.

Another culprit is a behavior problem or a psychiatric disorder that hinders a partner from carrying out his or her assigned duty as spouse and parent. It is important to realize that it's not necessarily the *divorce* that leads a youngster to go astray, but the *defect* of a parent that will or has, caused the divorce. Let's look into this hypothesis further.

It is known that a single-parent family in which one parent was taken away by death has fewer problems raising children than if the loss occurred through divorce. Before the death of the spouse, we assume that the family was fully functional as a two-parent unit, and after one dies the surviving parent does surprisingly well. This theory rests on the belief that a person who is capable of maintaining a good marriage is also competent in raising a family as a single parent.

We now take a case in which the partner in a two-parent setting becomes irrational and causes harm to the family. Many view this as more damaging than the death of a spouse or a divorce, and I support this finding. Let's observe such a family by looking through a kitchen window.

Trying to keep the family functional, the responsible spouse puts in double duty, but the ill partner sabotages the work by being demeaning and arrogant. He or she abuses the family in a controlling way, not realizing that this mannerism short-circuits all attempts to remedy the situation. Arguments break out, dishes get smashed, and the children cry. Counseling is of little help because the ill partner is unwilling or unable to change. The responsible spouse gets exhausted and a crisis situation is only a matter of time.

"Should a reasonable spouse hang on, or should he or she seek divorce to correct the home situation?" we ask. "What's more important, marriage or the family?" I agree with church leaders and counselors to restore the ailing marriage. If this has been tried, and there is no reason to believe that the situation will improve, divorce is the best choice. This decision should be made unencumbered by religious rules.

Keeping a malignant marriage alive against all odds is like feeding a tree with poison. It stifles growth and eventually causes death. The Latin proverb *Succisa virescit* (pruned, it grows again) also applies to families that have no hope of reconciliation. Clear and concise guidance from one parent is better than contradicting instructions from two. Just as we have two arms, two legs, two eyes, and two ears and are able to function with only one if the other is taken away, so also must the responsible parent make the tough call to go with one if the other becomes dysfunctional.

If divorce is inevitable, waiting for the children to grow up will have serious consequences, as my experience has shown. I confess that this realization came late for me also. I kept hoping for a miracle or a medical breakthrough. This didn't happen and biblical Lazarus did not awaken. Perhaps the biggest mental block was my conservative upbringing, believing that a marriage covenant is irrevocable, regardless of the circumstances involved. Yes, marriage should last for life, but there are exceptions. The ties *must* be broken if irresolvable marital problems harm the nucleus of the family. This view is in sharp contrast to my former belief that I so cherished.

When the horrible ordeal was over, I realized that God had given me a new lease on life. Although poorer in material things, I was now free to pursue my own goals. Most importantly, my family became functional again, albeit under the command of a single parent. My former wife could no longer blame me for her ups and downs. The reward of my hard work was now channeled toward the family and the money leak was plugged. My energy level and physical stamina improved and I no longer suffered from the persistent colds and flu symptoms that plagued me for a month at a time. Good health is vital when managing a demanding job—that of being a single parent.

I began realizing that *my divorce was the best gift I could give my children.* A dysfunctional two-parent family transformed into a functional single-parent family. The job of being a single parent was more manageable than I had first thought. With time, the children noticed the improvement and thanked me for the change. These words meant a lot to me. Being a single parent can be victorious. It can be fulfilling and rewarding.

There is a misconception that a single parent cannot do a fine job of raising a family, and statistical records supporting the ideas might be wrong. Allow me to repeat that it's not so much the *divorce* that causes youngsters to go astray, but the *human defect*, which leads to divorce. As good management is key to a flourishing business, so also does solid parenting build a functional and stable family. Although God's plan of a loving mother and father is best, the traditional family is not the only model that works. Success cannot be based on *marital status* alone but on the *character* and *competence* of the parent(s). Allow me to emphasize that God's original plan of a mother and father who are fully committed to marriage are the most qualified to do this job.

On my 10-km commute to work by bicycle I pass over a long bridge that crosses the Fraser River. Below is a large parking lot with smashed-up cars that are kept for insurance purposes. Observing these wrecks more closely, I noticed that many are fitted with fancy alloy wheels. One could conclude that the wheels were unsafe to drive and caused the car to crash. The assumption is wrong because the equation does not include the character of the driver. *Human behavior* is to blame rather than mechanics. In like manner, *parental competence* is key to a successful family and not marital status alone.

Going through a divorce and raising a family as a single parent doesn't automatically solve all problems. On the contrary! Like surgery the patient will likely get worse before better. This happened to us. Having dwelt in a dysfunctional family for more than five years, it was hard for the children to adapt to a more predictable home life. With their mother gone, they blamed me for everything that went wrong. I was the target of sharp criticism and became their punching bag, so to speak. It was their way of coping with the loss and they took out their frustrations on me.

Disrespectful behavior by youngsters is common in a divorce. The custodian parent must be aware and learn how to cope with this mannerism by being there and offering support. Who can better soak up the leaks from the hurting wounds of young children, and take the sharp hits from rebellious teenagers, than a loving parent?

We must look beyond the stinging remarks uttered and the insults flung and grasp the underlying cause. Youngsters want to check if parents are real, have integrity, and can be trusted. They want to make certain that Mom or Dad possesses the solid character that is required to lead the family through the troubled times. They push the limit, appear strong and in command, but deep inside they are broken, begging for sympathy and love.

As parents we must become a rock for them. We must exercise tolerance and understanding, while staying firm on delivery. Only by keeping a steady course, establishing solid household rules, and listening to their needs can a broken family become functional again. It took a full year before my family began adjusting to the new order, and the children began doing better with me in sole control.

How to Love a Teenager

There are times when raising a family seems like a thankless task. As a parent we pour so much love and care into what appears to be a leaky bucket, hoping to make a difference. All too soon we find out that the bucket can never be filled, even if we try to do our best. Much of the goodness is spilled and is seemingly lost in the arid ground. Lack of appreciation reaches climax point during the teenage years.

Raising children may go reasonably well until a youngster gets to be fourteen or so. Up till this moment a parent may say, "What's all the fuss about the teenage years everyone is talking about? I don't have these problems!" Then, all of a sudden, it hits them too. Established family rules fly out the window, and the youngsters test the parent's endurance in a direct and unrestrained way. "You don't understand me. I hate you, Mom!" they might yell, or, "You don't know anything. I can't stand you, Dad." A single parent has an especially tough time because he or she must endure the onslaught without the support of a partner.

Harsh words spoken to parents reflect a lack of respect and appreciation for the sacrifices made. It appears as if the teenagers want to disown the parents who have nurtured them. No matter how tough the situation gets, we as parent must continue to love and guide them. They are our inheritance. They are engraved on our hearts. They are all we have. We understand their feelings because we have been there too.

Teenage aggression finds its roots in the egocentric behavior of "me first." Youngsters want to challenge parental authority by establishing their own identity. I believe God programmed teenagers this way, enticing them to break away from the comfort of the nest and seek survival elsewhere. Parents must understand this transition as a necessary step for youngsters to become responsible adults. Getting married and having children of their own will divert the focus from their own selfish wants to helping others, first the spouse, then the children, and later the aging parents.

Rearing children, especially teenagers, is so unpredictable that only a *non-parent* can talk about it with confidence. The saying goes: *The best parents are the non-parents*. Once we become parents we are no longer so sure about ourselves. There is no book on parenting that provides all the answers. Each child is unique, and lessons learned for the first child won't necessarily apply for the other children.

A number of years ago, Charlie W. Shedd[16], a famous writer and speaker, titled his talk, "How to Raise Your Children." People came in droves and paid big money to hear him speak. Then the Shedds had children. It took him some time to get used to being a father, and from then on he spoke only occasionally on the family. He renamed the talk "Some Suggestions to Parents." Two more children arrived and Shedd seldom spoke on raising children. By now he had given his talk a third title: "Feeble Hints to Fellow Strugglers." After more children arrived Shedd addressed his audience by asking, "Anyone Here Got a Few Words of Wisdom?"

FUN BEING A PARENT

As unrewarding as raising youngsters may appear, the love given will pay back on its own timetable. One Father's Day not too long ago, I received a card from my son Perry, who had just married. The card read:

> Wanted: Dad. Long hours, little time off. Must be willing to work weekends, holidays and vacations. Energy, imagination, intelligence, understanding, endurance and flexibility required. Must have leadership qualities and the ability to instruct and guide, coupled with warm personality. On-the-job training offered. Thanks for taking the job, Dad. Happy Father's Day. *(With permission from Carlton Cards)*

The card included a handwritten thank-you note that said, "Your hard work at home and at the office goes mostly unnoticed. Your love, care, and support for your family is heartwarming to see." This note was especially meaningful coming from Perry because he was strong-willed and challenging to handle, particularly during his teenage years.

After my daughter, Holly, married and gave birth to her first child, she prepared a homemade Christmas card for me that I treasure to this day. It has twenty pages and carries the title "42 Reasons Why I Love You!" On brightly colored pages she drew funny family caricatures and added amusing word captions. The card tells the story of how she and her four younger brothers felt growing up in the busy Buchmann household. She later told me that this was her way of making up for the rough times she had given me during her teenage years, and to affirm her love to me.

I can't possibly list all 42 reasons. Some are just too embarrassing to mention. We clearly made a few boo-boos along the way, which our children will never forget. Kids have an amazingly good memory of what parents do wrong. By reading Holly's booklet again, I find that the word captions reflected our family situation spot-on. We were forever struggling, always in chaos, but still having lots of fun. Much of her writing reflects her younger years. She wrote:

> Dad, I love you for eating all the desserts I baked, even when nobody else would touch them . . .
>
> For not killing us kids when we cheered when you were pulled over by the police for speeding, or when the motor died . . .
>
> For teaching us to appreciate our minivan after being piled into the small sedan . . .
>
> For all the weekends of hard work you put into building the playhouse . . .
>
> For planting the blue spruce that now towers over the neighborhood . . .
>
> For being tolerant with our little pets, even when our house began to resemble Noah's Ark . . .

For cooking my favorite lunches of hash browns, eggs, and cheese when I came home for lunch . . .

For my piano lessons . . .

For scaling the house every year at our request to put up the Christmas lights . . .

For attending the Christmas plays at school . . .

For all the Christmas trees, even if the one we got was scrawny because it was the last one left . . .

For the Easter egg hunts and giving extra chocolates to the one who found the least . . .

For all the uphill rides home from Robert Burnaby Park . . .

For letting us use your workshop as a "Jungle Gym" . . .

For giving us your last french fry at Wendy's . . .

For all those "Smorgasbord Nights" when you tricked us into eating week-old leftovers, or making the stuff into "Swiss Soup" . . .

For all those bread ends you saved for us to feed the ducks after church . . .

For every bedtime story you read to me . . .

For teaching me how to drive, even if it was a terrifying experience . . .

For taking us to Paris, even if it meant dragging us across town . . .

For saying, "Hey, she looks like Holly," when you saw a model in a magazine . . .

For making me feel important by giving me my own office at Cadex . . .

For being able to fix absolutely anything that broke in the house.

The booklet finished off by wishing me a Merry Christmas, God's blessing, and lots of love. None of the wording hints at the growing difficulties in the family and their mother's intruding mental illness. The children were, for the most part, unencumbered and had fun.

They pulled their childish pranks, tested the boundaries, and expected to be punished for doing wrong. They saw the world at their eye level, shielded from the complex marital issues that gradually began unfolding.

Young children have the unique ability to mask a mild abnormality in the family and accept it as homegrown. Only when my youngsters became teenagers did they see that something was amiss. Their mother's strange behavior started to annoy them to no end and they didn't want to be seen with her in public.

Family problems entice youngsters to move out—often too soon. They want to detach themselves from an irritating parent to avoid arguments and embarrassments. Moving out prematurely attracts youngsters to the wrong crowd by hooking up with kids from other broken homes. Repairing the family fabric while the children are still young is paramount. Once the youngsters reach teenage years, it's often too late and the home setting tears like rotten fabric. I was pleased that Holly moved back home again after her mother left. She stayed with us until getting married.

Preparing the youngster for the journey of life can be compared to assembling the cars of a freight train for the long journey. The parents must arrange the rolling stock in the right order while the train stays at the home yard. When the teenage years arrive, we set the switches, post the speed limit, and give the green light. As parents we must realize that the engines are now hot and revved up, ready to go. The rolling stock is about to move on its own power. Once in motion, the train cannot easily be stopped, much less the cars rearranged. We must stand back and allow the train to pass, lest we get run over. Waving arms and yelling will do little at this time. The sound of the engines will drown out the hollering. Although seemingly powerless at this stage, we can *pray* that the train will keep its posted speed limit so that the cars won't derail and spill the load.

To the secular society, marriage is convenience, a social vessel in which to navigate. When the relationship fails, the couple splits up and regroups. Religion mandates that a marriage be permanent with no exit. I view marriage as the foundation on which to build a family, with parental responsibility to dissolve the union if internal discord causes harm.

CHAPTER 12

TEENAGE YEARS

FINANCIAL RESPONSIBILITY

Teenagers are opportunists and know how the cookie crumbles. They test the boundaries and bend the rules to see how far they can go. I heard mine say, "If I don't get it from Dad, I'll get it from Mom." And they did! The problems started before the divorce and carried on afterward.

Turning 16, my boys wanted cars very much. Since I was against lending money for this, they asked their mother. Trying to please, she gave in. After all, she had the money—tons of it. With the transfer of my life savings and the sale of the houses as part of the divorce settlement, my "ex" became wealthy overnight. With this newly acquired prosperity and the freedom to spend it unencumbered, she became a gold mine from which the boys could satisfy their every desire. First came the fancy sports cars, and when the excitement and exhilaration of speed wore off, they wanted large motorcycles, and got them too.

The wasteful spending annoyed me to no end. I felt as if someone had thrust a knife through my chest. I saw the hard-earned money being squandered virtually overnight. I had no power to stop the carnage. I came to Canada with only a hundred dollars in my pocket, worked myself through low-paying jobs, drove old cars, and built the family house myself to save money. Our prudent lifestyle eventually enabled a comfortable life, for which we were grateful. But the divorce opened the floodgates and dissipated what took a lifetime to build. I pleaded with Sophie to stop, only to be ignored and ridiculed. I couldn't restrain my teenagers either. What youngster would walk away from a resource that flowed so freely?

What worried me most was the safety of the boys. The fast motorcycles were my biggest concern. They participated in many challenging races, and I wondered if I would ever see them in one piece and alive again. All I could do was pray. Their cars did get smashed and the motorcycle twisted, but the boys survived with only cuts and bruises.

Money is a powerful force that can afflict great harm if used unwisely. I didn't want my children to become slaves to materialism. Always getting what they wanted was the quickest way to becoming enslaved to greed and covetousness. How could I teach the youngsters the reward of hard work if their dreams were fulfilled for free? They had their shiny sports cars and racy motorcycles before turning twenty without getting a drop of sweat on their brow. My son boasted, "I could drive circles around your old minivan," and yes, he could. I was less interested in horsepower and agility than in instilling respect and appreciation for money earned through honest labor.

It was most unfortunate that the judge didn't listen to my divorce lawyer, who proposed setting up a trust fund that would release money to Sophie as needed. The judge brushed off this suggestion as being unnecessary. Many judges do only what's mandated, namely authorize the divorce, divide the personal belongings, and assign a custodian for the children. Job done. The consequences that might come as result of a careless court decision seem less important to them.

Sophie's wealth soon faded. Broke and in serious debt, she requested that I buy her share of the family home before the allotted time. Paying her out helped for a while, but she soon slipped into debt again.

Wisdom escapes me why we couldn't set up a trust fund this time that would have managed her new assets and controlled the spending. Declaring her mentally incapable with finances while managing her own apartment was, however, too difficult. No doctor would sign the legal papers to declare her incapacitated. As it happens all too often, systems have cracks and those falling into them have little wiggle room to escape.

Unable to pay her newly acquired debt, the only available choice was to sell her stately two-bedroom condominium with the new furniture and move into a cramped government-subsidized suite. As she kept spending using numerous credit cards with no means to pay back, she finally had to declare bankruptcy.

With the money gone, a rift formed between the older boys, who had received liberal handouts, and the two younger ones, who weren't part of the bonanza. The younger ones began accusing their older brothers of having misused the trust of their ill mother. We organized a family meeting and agreed that the money must be paid back. Today, this fund provides an extra living allowance for their needy mother. The younger boys were wise by keeping their hands out of the cookie jar.

I am certain that Sophie meant well by giving money to the youngsters. It was a way of extending her love, hoping that the children would visit her more often. As with many families, this only worked as long as there were cookies in the jar. Times have improved, and today my children see beyond the lure of money and visit their mother often.

Money can become an adversary to families, especially if mismanaged. Passing wealth to the next generation must be done in an orderly and organized way. Succession planning should start early, and each sibling should be informed of his or her part of the family assets. Families that offer love as inheritance often do better and form stronger family ties than those who build their future on material wealth alone.

PERRY'S LETTER

What should a parent do when a teenager becomes stubborn, defiant, and doesn't want to take advice? Should Mom and Dad insist on finding a solution then and there, or would it be better to allow the storm to ride out? The never-ending arguments with my wife taught me to stay out trouble and I often walked away. This shortcut backfired and my teenagers called me a "cop-out."

A sensible action for a parent when in disputes with a youngster is admitting that no immediate solution is at hand, and then set a date for a future discussion. More often than not, the teenager doesn't want to rehash the issue at the appointed time, and in this case the argument was in the heat of the moment, an aggravation that cooled off with time.

If I could do it over again, I would attempt (not force) to communicate with my teenagers and tell them that I loved them. I would show respect and give praise for any small deeds they did, and then allow the issue to settle on its own timetable. If no communication were possible on that day, this would be fine too. There would always be a better day coming.

Offering approval for a job well done is an excellent way to open an angry and disgruntled heart. Equally important is providing the youngster with a pleasant home environment by keeping plenty of food in the refrigerator for them to help themselves. Asking if they're hungry when they come in, and then preparing a meal just for them, is an excellent way to bond with teenagers. This shows that they always have a welcoming place to come home to. Good deeds rather than words pass the message of love and acceptance, and the stomach is one of the best receptors, even if such indulgence will spoil the youngster for a season.

When Perry was 19, communication was difficult and he withdrew. Nothing pleased him, or so it seemed. He brushed off and ridiculed all of my suggestion as unworkable. He preferred associating with his friends, especially Ram, with whom he could vent his frustrations. One day I received an e-mail from Perry that disturbed me. The message was also copied to Ram and read:

Hi Dad,

Since you are too hard to talk to, I write my feelings in an e-mail. Lately, we haven't been getting along. I feel you are giving me a hard time about everything. You are trying to teach me some "life's rules" when there is really no point in doing this. I am old enough, and "playing father" when it's too late is wasting both our time. I find myself almost hating you. Let's face it, you do absolutely nothing for me. I mean that in every sense of the word. I have places I can stay and can get money at will.

I soon received a follow-up e-mail from Ram, who wrote, "Wow, quite an explosive e-mail Perry sent you! I didn't know he was that angry." He then gave his own opinion of my parenting style and wrote:

> I really don't know what you do for Perry that he should be thankful for. You did not help him at all when it came to his car. You were against Perry getting a Porsche. You don't want to give your children any kind of money to spend to help them select cars.

Ram has Indian roots and his parents exercise an Eastern culture in which family members share the common assets. The money is put on the table and everyone can take what he or she needs, with certain limits attached. This philosophy is as far from my European upbringing as East is from the West. It's my strong conviction that a teenager should *earn* his money to buy a car. A loan should only be given if the youngster can present a viable payback plan. How else can a parent teach that material possession doesn't come for free but has a price?

I had always thought that things were going pretty well with Perry (more or less). I knew that a teenager wants to keep autonomy, especially if no parental support had been sought. It was as if Perry had drawn his shades and put up a sign that read "Do not disturb." Like most fathers, I didn't want to probe into his personal affairs unless asked. For the most part, a father dislikes long discussions, especially if they touch on feelings, or family issues that cannot be changed. I only fix stuff that is broken, and I didn't want to take something apart that appeared to be running. I realize now that a few drops of oil on the grinding wheels would have done wonders. A serious talk with my son was long overdue.

Research by Motorola Canada confirms that discussions between parents and teenager are often strained. The study reveals that teenagers don't want to talk about their problems, especially not to their fathers. The youngsters are embarrassed to open up and are afraid of being labeled "weird" or "abnormal." Those willing to talk want to share their hurts and anxieties with their friends rather than parents. The study found that 42 percent of teens rarely, or never, ask for help when feeling overwhelmed, 67 percent turn to their friends, 60 percent to their moms and only 32 percent to their dads or siblings. When it comes to discussing feelings, mothers do a better job than fathers.

Did Perry's anger arise because I refused to lend him money to buy the Porsche after the motor of his Talon started burning oil? Or was there a deeper cause? Could this dispute have been avoided had I made an effort to better communicate with him? Would a loving mother have helped?

I didn't want to leave this question unanswered and I finally asked Perry for an answer. Being older now, he said that although the car was important, this wasn't the main reason. When pressed for a response, and listening for keywords, he finally admitted that he couldn't give me a clear explanation. He was embarrassed to talk about the past and wanted closure. I understood his desire and called it quits. This era is now a distant memory, water under the bridge, a closed book. At least that's what I thought.

As part of writing this book, I asked Perry to review the chapter containing his e-mail. It opened up old wounds. Happily married and living in his own house, he expressed surprise at the harsh words he had written. His outlook on life has changed and he has adopted a more prudent lifestyle. He traded his Porsche for a compact four-door Honda Civic with half the horsepower. What touched me the most was the e-mail that followed. E-mail is a great media, especially if one wants to open up and get a little sentimental without making eye contact. Perry wrote:

> Hi Dad,
>
> This is a very touching story and I get emotional as I empathize with what we were going through. What you accomplished is simply amazing. Well done! You had a lot on your plate and you seemed to do exceptionally well in all of the important areas. Never mind the kitchen not being sterilized, the garage messy, and closet doors left partially open. The family has been raised with good values, an impeccable sense of survival, and most importantly, lots of love and respect for each other.

Thinking back to my tough teenage years, we were both trying to figure out how to interact with each other while maintaining our pride and keeping our priorities straight. Yes, I do remember writing that specific e-mail. The intent was not to put you down, but to reach out for your acceptance and verbal involvement. Deep inside, I was crying for help. There wasn't much communication back then. I am improving now. I know for sure that I acted like an ass at times, probably the majority of the time. So for all those mean things I said, the disrespect and lack of appreciation I showed, I want to say I'm sorry.

I understand now that you didn't want me to become a materialistic, show-off kind of jerk—and believe me, I was well down that path at 19. Your struggles, hurts, silent disapprovals, and the long walks you took at night, finally sunk in and prompted me to grow up. Just so you are aware, I don't feel resentment or have any grudges about how I grew up. The path was rocky for everyone and the circumstances were less than ideal. I found your leadership fair. I still remember your one-liner to my complaints that still ring in my ears. You simply said, "Life isn't fair."

I appreciate how you allowed us kids to create our own economy within the household. You instilled the worth of money, taught business sense, and insisted on following set family rules. This fostered sharpness for business and respect for the law. I appreciate having received this tool kit; it comes in handy now.

When I stopped by your house a few months ago, Holly (who lives in the basement suite with her husband and children) gave me the compliment of all compliments. She said, "Holy Perry, you are more and more like Dad; you are even beginning to look like him." Holly and I talk over the phone every now and then about our childhood. I find these conversations an emotional roller coaster. We also spoke about the book you are writing and how much of a tough time we gave you during "wandering" years.

Yes, we should improve our communication, but it's awkward to talk about feelings. It's a funny thing with us boys; we are built to be strong and not to express our vulnerability. I feel that expressing my feelings reveals a weakness in me. My wife is amazing and she truly helps in completing me, especially emotionally.

You said it best by explaining that rather than refining our manners, we struggled for survival. It's not a surprise that the Buchmanns have some polishing to do. It's different now. We are blessed with material things and no longer need to dwell in survival mode.

I want you to know that I love you very much. I look up to you and have an unparalleled respect for you that I do not have with anyone else in this world. I try to emulate what you stand for at work. I ask God to bless me with your traits as I feel it will make me great like you.

I love you, Dad.

Perry

I get emotional each time I read this letter again. For a while, I had thought that my teachings had gone nowhere, but Perry's writing confirms that my words were absorbed during the dry spell. A foundation was being built underground that could not be seen from street level. This very foundation is now becoming the underpinning for a new generation, a building that arises above ground and stands big and strong.

In my desire to bring the letter writing to a close, I also contacted Ram by sending him this same chapter of the book to read. I wanted to know if his view had changed, now that he was older. Ram is a very intelligent young man, holds a manager position, and studies in Toronto for his master's degree. He wrote me the following letter:

Hello Isidor,

I've read the draft and enjoyed it tremendously, but there is a heavy weight on my shoulders. I apologize for having attempted to bring materialism into your family. I am troubled by the thought of enticing Perry to become like me, a materialistic, show-off kind of jerk.

I seem to attract people from broken families, those looking for a father figure, but I don't have the wisdom or experience to be that person because of my young age. I may have cheated Perry by filling this position even though he had a much richer experience, that of his own dad.

I cannot imagine how it felt reading my notes in which I hinted that you were "doing nothing for which Perry should be thankful for," or in "not helping him buy an expensive sports car." I am disgusted with myself for writing this. It shows my immaturity and stupidity during that time. I don't know what else I can say besides, I'm sorry. I can tell you that I've learned much from you and I have a high respect for you, on par with that of my own mother and father. I also appreciate your teachings. In fact, one of your phrases I like the most is, "Life isn't fair."

The friendship with Perry was a big boost for me. He taught me how to improve my self-confidence and to treat people better.

Take care,
Ram

If nothing else does, these words bring closure. The difficult teenage years will pass, and a more predictable and mature thinking pattern will emerge. Youngsters who go through great tribulations during the teenage years often become stronger adults and achieve greater success in life than the more complacent folks. A child who was challenging to rear often surprises the parents later in life with strong determination and endurance, key ingredients for a successful career.

LEAVING THE NEST

God lends us the children for only a season. When the time comes to move out, the young will pack up and leave. Even though raising the troop was hard, this is a difficult time for parents. We dislike spillage and want to keep the nest full.

Raising children is like waiting at a railway crossing while a long freight train slowly passes by. The unscheduled stop is always an inconvenience because we had planned the day differently. The delay this morning seems extra long. We are impatient and can't wait to get to the other side of the tracks to carry out our planned mission. We start counting the passing cars but soon get distracted. Then, finally, the last car is in sight, passes quickly, disappears down the track, and the train is gone. The track is clear.

We check our watch and notice that thirty years have passed. The surroundings have become quiet and we are suddenly all alone. Our intended mission is now a blur and no longer important. We decide to turn around and go home. But instead of entering a house bustling with active children, we find an empty place. We sit in a quiet room, our mind still following the train, wondering where it's heading and how far it has traveled. Loneliness sets in and we hope that one of the kids will call to say hello.

Every parent will eventually experience the bittersweet moment when he or she will sit in a quiet room and stare at the marks on the wall left behind as souvenirs of a busy household. How we wish that the happy voices would return one more time! For a while it appeared that raising a family was a never-ending chore that would take a lifetime—and now this time has shrunk to a short season.

We look back at the stage where the family played and watch the scenes unfolding. They are etched in stone that can no longer be changed, although at times we wish we could. God gave us only one season to perform our parental duty, and that opportunity has now passed. We reminisce on the good times and try to forget the less desirable moments. Each family has a bit of both.

For those going through rough times raising a family, let me assure you that quieter times will lie ahead. Just as tending a garden during the hot and dry summer produces little in return until autumn, so also do parents see only thorns and thistle when the youngsters go through the parched teenage years. When the replenishing rains come and the refreshing water quenches the earth, the flowers burst into bloom, the fruits explode with sweetness, and life receives its reward.

It's reassuring to know that there is a God who understands our problems and accepts who we are. In due time, the heavens will send relief to all struggling families and the difficult times will pass. It's then when the young adult will discover the valuable treasure that lays hidden in the family chest. The work put in by the parents will come to light and turn into a precious asset, rising above material possessions. The everyday quandaries will be forgotten, and the thorny issues will no longer consume us as they did then. This is the time when we begin realizing that divine help was at work to guide the family through the rough passage.

Theodore Roosevelt, a professional historian, naturalist, explorer, hunter, author, soldier, and president of the United States placed the work of a parent above his own achievements and writes:

> No other success in life—not being president, or being wealthy, or going to college, or writing a book, or anything else—comes up to the success of the man or woman who can feel that they have done their duty, and that their children and grandchildren rise up and call them blessed.
>
> —Theodore Roosevelt, 1917

Marriage is built on the understanding that both parties are rational and mature. *Divorce for just cause* is poorly understood in Christian circles and those leaving an irrational spouse often face judgment. God is less concerned with rules than harmony and a stable home.

CHAPTER 13

IN THE EYES OF THE CHILDREN

In preparation of this book, I asked my children to write their own stories on how they felt growing up during the turbulent years and how the family crisis has affected them personally. When we are entwined in the depth of problems we are less aware of what's happening around us. We see the damage only after the storm has passed and calm has returned. More than twelve years have elapsed since Sophie left our family and we have had plenty of time to reflect.

Randy, our youngest, will tell his story first. His is the shortest because he remembers the least of the family crisis. We then proceed to the older boys and finish with Holly, who has the most to say. Her writing is more like a lamentation than a story, reflecting her silent suffering living at home. Being the only girl, she had the disadvantage of growing up in a male-dominated boot camp that was fast-paced and goal-oriented. I appreciate her honesty and outspokenness.

Although writing the stories brings back old memories, the exercise has helped heal our wounds. Never before have we exchanged our feelings so openly and freely than over a home-cooked meal around the family table. Sharing our personal experiences is a good way to bring closure to the past. The stories my children wrote are presented in their original form with some editing for length and clarity.

RANDY'S STORY

(20 at time of writing; six when his mother left)

My childhood memories started when we were living in the house my dad built. It was often chaotic and loud. Most of my toddler years were quite pleasant. Because I was the baby in the family, my mom used to give me whatever I wanted.

After we moved into the new house, it was clear that my parents were not getting along. They separated soon after and I was only allowed to see my mom once a week. After the divorce, I spent time with my brothers and friends and did not pay too much attention to the divorce. My dad told me that my mom was sick and I understood that. My childhood was hectic. This was caused by sibling rivalry and my taking part in the many activities of my older brothers. I followed them blindly and did what I was told to do.

I recall a memory in kindergarten. I was eating lunch with my friends and we were arguing as to who had the best father. I said I did, and stubbornly argued to the end. I always thought my dad was perfect, even though my relationship with him was quite distant. The little time I spent with Dad was when we did chores, or when he tucked us boys into bed and read stories to us.

I didn't get much guidance during my childhood years. I learned my way mostly by observing what my older siblings did. The little guidance I did get from my parents was about having good morals. I have sometimes broken those principles and have felt guilty in doing so.

As the youngest of five, I respected the actions of my older siblings and always tried to please them, but many times they took advantage of this. Todd and I had to listen to Mattie and Perry's orders and sometimes we did inappropriate things. We felt we had no other choice than to obey or else we would be beaten up. It was rare that I told Dad my problems—nothing would get resolved anyway. There was simply not enough supervision in our family to keep the older siblings from harassing the younger ones. Going through all these experiences gave me a short temper and a competitive nature. I still carry these traits in me.

I am aware of my mother's condition. After the divorce, I kept in close contact with her through weekly visits and numerous phone calls. She has an incredibly caring nature and possesses a worrying manner, a quality I enjoy. I got to know my dad better on a personal level by spending more time with him and sharing opinions. Over the years, my relationship with my siblings also matured. Holly gave me her big-sister advice and taught me new ways to cook. Perry and I shared the same hobbies and we always competed to bring out the best in each other. Mattie was always the most fun to be around because one never knew what he would do next. Todd's constant motivation pushes me to be better.

The divorce left Dad with no other choice than to let us raise ourselves. He put food on the table, but didn't have much time to devote to each of us. I have no hard feelings toward any of my family members and I am glad that we are now closely knit together. I feel very blessed that our family is strong and united.

I give most credit to my dad for keeping the family together. He never broke down and persistently gave all he could to make us happy, even though he had limited time to raise us. I look at him as my role model because he leads by example, is strong willed, and is smart.

TODD'S STORY

(22 at time of writing; eight when his mother left)

The divorce of my parents was not devastating for me. I accepted the reality and thought little about it. My early childhood is filled with many fond memories of growing up. I remember playing in the back-yard, picking delicious plums and cherries off our fruit trees, going for family walks, and playing in the park across the street with the neighborhood kids. Life at home gave me a carefree environment with plenty of food on the table. Some of the more serious problems only arose as we grew older.

My less-fond memories began after moving into the new house next door. The family started to go downhill from there. It began with the difficult teenage years of Holly and Perry, then 15 and 12. Holly was usually out of the house and spent excessive time with friends. She transferred from school to school and stayed with another family. But Perry's strong-willed attitude created the biggest problems.

After Mom moved out of the house, two separate societies emerged: Dad's society was based on the example of good ethics and morals, but we lived under Perry's "secret society." I call it a secret society because nobody other than us boys knew what was going on.

Perry was the uncontested leader. He was the oldest, the strongest, and perceived to be the wisest among us boys. Naturally, his younger siblings looked up to him as a role model. He struck fear in us boys through intimidation and made Randy and me his "servants." I frequently went for daylong bicycle trips just to get out of the house and away from him.

I tried to seek Dad's protection but he would downplay the situation. He had his own problems and could not be bothered with mine. As a result, the "slavery" continued. I felt Dad did not care about my problems and wouldn't listen. We only got his attention when we broke something in the house or made a mess in the kitchen. I went from being a sensitive and naïve boy to being thick-skinned. I grew up faster than most kids my age and adopted an aggressive behavior that has carried on to this day.

In elementary school I was often sent to the principal's office for aggressive behavior and for annoying the teachers. Later, in high school, some kids called me names. At first I took the abuse in stride and bottled it up. Then, all of the sudden, it reached a boiling point and I got into several fistfights. These incidents gave me a bad reputation.

I was very competitive in sports and my temper would often get the best of me. Always wanting to give 100 percent effort, I would get frustrated if my team lost. I would get into quarrels and sometimes punched a player from the other team in sheer frustration.

I think the best thing Dad did in raising me was sending me to a good Catholic school. With limited supervision at home, my elementary school teachers acted as parental figures. This guidance played a key role because they would discipline me for my bad behavior. Coaches, teachers, and my personal trainer were my mentors. I respected them and looked up to them in getting direction.

Dad adapted a unique style of child raising by laying a solid foundation and then leaving us kids in the hands of God and letting us go free. He always hoped for the best. With minimal parental input, letting me expose myself to the real world, and letting me learn through my own mistakes made me a wiser person. The Buchmann kids must have had some very dedicated guardian angels.

I cannot blame Dad for the way he ran the household. He had an enormous task, raising five children and running a company without losing his sanity. Dad made up for his shortcomings as a father by giving solid advice and always leading by example. He never strayed from being an honest hardworking person. Sometimes, I wonder if he ever sleeps in on weekends. He never lies and always keeps his promises. I still look up to Dad as a small child would and I see him as a rock, strong and honest. He stands up for his beliefs.

I do not remember my mother's presence much because she left when I was eight. I knew her mostly as living outside the home. I feel sympathy for her because she had a difficult time after leaving the family and moving to her sister's house in Langley. She could only see us once a week. A few years later, she purchased her own condominium, but squandered the money in a few years and then declared bankruptcy.

I think my mom realizes that she missed a large part of my life and is now trying to make it up. She frequently travels two hours by bus to visit us for only a few hours. She is very generous and would give us the world if she could. Even though I am a young adult now, Mom still tries to give me advice, as if I were thirteen years old. She sends me nice cards and photos in the mail just to say hello and provide support. Her warm and affectionate nature is a nice contrast to my dad, who is more of a businessman and straight to the point.

My family life is now balanced and happy, and my mom is content with her new life. She is independent and still has close ties with us, including the new grandchildren. My dad is happy being the owner and CEO of a successful business. Even though our family has been through many highs and lows, God has blessed us dearly. I do not feel any shame about our past.

Mattie's Story

(24 at time of writing; ten when his mother left)

My dad asked me to write a short story about the experiences of my childhood. Although I know it was very challenging at times, I can't help but wonder why anyone would want to read this. Somehow, I seemed to have survived, so I'm sure it couldn't have been all that bad.

Most of my early childhood memories revolve around my sister, Holly. At a young age, she took a liking to me and would include me in her dress-up plays with her dolls, tea parties, and eventually she compelled me to watch scary movies with her. She must have matured at twice the rate of her friends. I mean, she was basically raising the Buchmann boys.

From the time I was barely old enough to walk, Holly was a mother figure and I escaped the pressure of being in constant competition with my brothers. Perry was the undisputed leader. He formulated plans utilizing his existing army (his brothers). Of course, he was at the top and operated by using cheap labor!

My elementary years were filled with the struggles of feeling un-accepted. I was always able to read and speak well, but had a hard time with basic arithmetic. I was too nervous to say anything for fear someone might think I was stupid.

Around that time, Perry was entering his teenage years and he began to make a name for himself. He started getting into trouble with other classmates and was suspended three times. I remember him boasting, "I got suspended this many times; let's see how well you can do at it." From that point on, I worked hard at fighting back against anyone who purposely defied me. My grades continued to suffer, and when I graduated from elementary school, I had been suspended seven times. Was I proud of this? Probably not!

I remember one specific incident on a cold winter morning in grade five or six when a young girl whipped her jacket across my face. I lost my temper, grabbed her by the hair, and struck her twice. It didn't matter to me if it was a boy or girl. If someone hurt me, they would get it right back. After this episode, I was in and out of the principal's office and saw many student counselors.

Entering high school, my number one goal was to make a name for our family. I wanted to build respect to pave the way for my younger brothers. By doing so, I tried to instill the creed that *messing with a Buchmann wouldn't go unpunished*. I was very competitive in high school, and sports were a natural outlet.

Then, it happened in grade eleven. I was suspended from school for one week for bullying a classmate. For some unknown reason, I picked on this fellow. He had blonde hair and blue eyes and was stocky. Every time I saw him, I physically or mentally abused him. One day, something came over me. I saw him in the hallway, grabbed him by the collar, and repeatedly slammed him against the wall until my knuckles were bleeding. The principal was keen to expel me from school and recommended police charges. He thought that this assault was outside the school's discipline, and my dad was called in to talk to the principal.

During that week at home alone, I had time to reflect. Until now, I was always told what to do, when, where, and how. I hated school with a passion, or at least I thought I did. As the days passed, I worried that the school did not want me back. I had good friends there and was eager to return and finish high school. After my dad spoke with the principal, something happened and I was allowed back.

Throughout my high school years, I was in and out of the school counselor's office. My ability to express myself verbally served as an advantage. My dad always told me that I would become a good salesman. Seeing counselors was great because it gave me an excuse to stay out of class for an hour. I would say what they wanted to hear to make them feel that they had made progress with me.

Rock bottom came after I graduated from high school. My friends and I walked into a fast-food restaurant to grab something to eat. We wanted to bring the provisions down to the beach and watch the annual fireworks at English Bay in Vancouver. The weather was humid and everyone in line was restless to get a good spot at the beach. Then, a young woman accused us of cutting into the line. After ignoring her, she became aggressive and raised her voice. She called her boyfriend over, who subsequently flashed gang signs. I needed to stand my ground and mouthed off to the rival as I proceeded toward the door. There, I spotted an empty glass bottle, grabbed it, and threw it back at the assailant as hard as I could. The next few moments of my life became a blur. Mug shots, fingerprints, and a night in a jail cell gave me a good opportunity to rethink my action.

I find writing about my mother most difficult. Today, she loves me deeply and would sacrifice her own happiness for mine. She would even travel two hours by public transit just to spend the night in my apartment. We cook together and talk about the past. Her love knows no boundaries. I can say that it wasn't always this way.

My mother was a very different person when I was a child and her personality was somewhat aloof. She seemed only interested in herself and had a short temper when provoked. Before she left, she seemed to have taken her frustrations out on me for some unknown reasons. Perhaps I did not listen to her, or I might have been an easy target. I will not get into specifics of the physical abuse I received; but I believe that it was one of the reasons why I had difficulty developing good relationships with teachers, classmates, and girlfriends.

I don't blame Mom or Dad for the way my siblings and I were raised. My mother was mentally ill and according to her, Dad was a workaholic. I wouldn't know because he was never around. I would say that I probably didn't grow up in the best conditions, but I think this has helped us in appreciating what we have today. It has built a strong family bond that is continuing to this day.

PERRY'S STORY

(27 at time of writing; 13 when his mother left)

Growing up was a challenging experience for us all. During our younger years, we kids didn't realize that the family was in survival mode. I thought this was normal and I am sure my siblings shared my view. The challenge was getting through the day. Every scrap of food, every second of time, and every penny counted, even at the expense of the quality of life. Our fundamentals were in line with any Catholic family: *Don't steal, share with your siblings, and treat elders with respect.* Although we didn't always follow the rules, we definitely felt guilty when we broke them.

Mom was caring and loving; she was a strangely generous lady but had a serious mean streak. At the end, she did whatever she pleased. If anyone asked about Mom now, we would likely praise her, although we all agree that she was impossible to live with. She was not nice to Dad and did certain things to make him angry. As a child, I asked her why she wanted to make Dad so mad. She said, "He is a bad man," or "He is having an affair." Whenever we heard this, we would instantly stand up for Dad. We all knew that her accusations were far from the truth. Although bothersome to Dad, her comments rolled off our backs with no side effects.

The family ran like a business with no human resources department. All of us kids knew how to secure the basic human needs. We all possessed little in material goods, but Mom was quite generous with her favorite kid of the week. We bartered or traded our possessions for other things of value. It was really the younger ones who suffered, as they didn't realize the market value of their things. Holly, Mattie, and I usually came out on top in any transaction. But that didn't last too long. Todd and Randy were quick to catch up.

Nothing was better than being Mom's favorite kid of the week. At random, she would bring one of the kids on her shopping binges to the mall in New Westminster. One day I scored a new pair of Nike shoes and a skateboard, and it wasn't even my birthday! The shock and excitement was indescribable. That night, I remember staring at the bedroom ceiling trying to figure out why I had been so lucky. The sudden injection of material things did not go unnoticed in the household; everyone resented me for this—even Dad.

We knew that Mom's spending habits worried Dad. Although he voiced concerns, no one wanted to alter Mom's money policy. "What benefit would this be for us?" we asked. We all received a gift from Mom at some point, but never felt right taking it. We were always instructed to hide the gifts from Dad. Todd was the first to reject the gifts and demanded that she save the money instead. We were quite shocked and unprepared to adopt such rules.

As time went on, home life became less and less pleasant. There was much tension between Mom and Dad, and Mom and us kids. Holly and I would spend as much time as possible away from home, staying at our friends' houses. I recall several of Mom's nervous breakdowns. One time, the police showed up at our house. I also remember traveling to Los Angeles when Mom disappeared during a restaurant meal, wandered off into a deserted field, and broke down in front of our eyes. On the way home, while leaving the motel in Oregon in the morning, she braced herself against the exit door and screamed for someone to make us stop. We forced her against her will by carrying her to the minivan. I'm sure this didn't look good to the other guests. She resisted help from anyone. There was a sigh of relief when she was ordered to leave our home. The fighting stopped and she got the much-needed care she deserved.

We visited Mom at various hospitals. The drugs produced strange nervous side effects. She would be sluggish and zoned out; she would continuously keep her mouth open and move her leg or hands in a fidgety manner. This was hard for us to take. After all, she was our dear mother. She eventually stabilized, but still needs medication. She is now self-sufficient, lives on her own, and fills her days with hobbies. All of us love Mom dearly.

What we missed growing up was parental involvement, communication, validation, and acceptance. A small list, but this void created a huge psychological gap. All of us had trouble with the law. This was not just breaking household rules, but civil laws. At some point, one or more of us stole belongings, vandalized objects, threatened others, assaulted, extorted, and abused individuals inside and outside the home. Our motives were based on getting personal gain, some were revenge, others gaining power.

If I were asked what could have prevented me from breaking the law, I would say more parental involvement and guidance. Did my parents know what we were up to behind their backs? I don't know. I am sure if Dad had known the severity of the offenses, he would have stepped in to set us straight. I got a few lickings for other stuff he discovered. Would better guidance and communication have solved this? Yes, but it was hard to implement when the family was dysfunctional.

Looking back, I have mixed emotions about my childhood. The good thing is that Mom and Dad are laughing again. The experience with a mentally ill mother made us more tolerant of the infirmities of others. My biggest blessing is my wife. She is my strength and stability; she allows me to look back with understanding eyes.

HOLLY'S STORY

(30 at time of writing; 16 when her mother left)

"It must be really hard for you, Holly." I heard this phrase over and over again from my aunts and family friends who empathized with my role as the eldest daughter of five kids in the midst of family disharmony. At the age of ten, I never thought of myself as having an extraordinarily hard life, but I was aware of my duties to babysit my four younger brothers, change diapers, prepare bottles, and do the weekly housecleaning.

As children, we loved our household. We were never questioned or held accountable, and discipline easily slipped through the grasp of our many nanny-housekeepers (God bless every one of them). We always had plenty of playmates. Everyone wanted to play at our house because something interesting was always happening there. We had a big wooded yard, a Scooby Doo pool, a beautiful playhouse that Dad built, a swing set, another swing hanging from the plum tree, a trampoline, and plenty of things to dig up in Dad's vegetable garden. Summertime was heavenly bliss for a child in our home.

When we were still young, we found refuge in one another's company. We were a civilization of five with a faithful nanny who picked up after us and fed our bellies. Our play and laughter muffled the noise of Mom's and Dad's bickering. As we grew old enough to understand the nature of the arguments, we always sided with my dad, whom we felt was the wiser one. Mom's family began to involve themselves and openly accused Dad in front of us kids. These remarks would deeply offend us children and we stood terribly loyal to Dad.

In grade four, my parents placed me in a new school and the adjustment, coupled with my home life, weighed heavily on me emotionally. I was under peer scrutiny with a small clique of Filipina girls. They were quick to point out the strange, tight evening dresses my mom would wear to Sunday church. Of course, this brought to my awareness that my mom was different from the other mothers at school and that other people were noticing. Before long, I was known as the "girl who cries every day at school." Indeed, I did, and teachers were beginning to question my home environment.

When I was 14, I came down with the worst case of stomach flu imaginable and missed two weeks of school. I felt so weak that my days consisted of sleeping, waking up, and then walking ten steps to my father's side of their queen-sized bed. Dad wanted to make a doctor's appointment, but Mom burst into the room and created a big drama. "Look at me!" she ridiculed, "I am Holly. I am sooo sick, boo-hoo . . ." She figured I was pretending to be sick to get the attention of my father. I didn't really expect much from my mother, but that day I felt completely victimized. My father told me to pay no attention to her.

I simply couldn't stand my mother, much less to be around her. On a shopping trip with her, she'd insist on staying at the mall to see the movie my girlfriend and I had planned to watch *alone*! If I bought a shirt I liked, she would go out the next day and buy the same shirt from the same store in all available colors and extra-large sizes. Not only would this irritate me beyond belief, it would make me want to burn my own shirt.

She regularly called the mothers of my girlfriends and told them elaborate stories that were fictional. Our trip to Disneyland was especially hard. At the hotel, she banged on the door of a big African-American family, insisting that she heard her 15-year old daughter inside. Later, she informed her childhood friend, whom she visited in Anaheim, that I was sneaking out at night and going to bars with strange men. All this was completely untrue. The final breakdown gave me a sense of relief that some change would be happening soon.

When I was 16, my best friend invited me to travel to India with her family for a vacation. I leapt at the opportunity to escape and spent six weeks at their family compound in Punjab. Halfway through my trip, the hosts encouraged me to call home to tell my dad that I was OK. We went to the main village and made the call from a little long-distance phone business with a tented roof on a dirt street. When I recognized my dad's voice, I burst into tears, overcome by emotions. I became inaudible and lost my composure. After a brief conversation, I hung up, my eyes red and swollen as big as saucers. It suddenly occurred to me that after escaping the difficult family situation, I didn't belong anywhere.

Returning home, I decided to give more effort to my home life. I started getting A's again on my report card and adopted a more positive outlook. By this time, my parents were separated and my mother was living in Langley with her sister. My dad was doing his best to cope with his new role as a single parent.

Cadex began to do better and Dad took my two youngest brothers and me to Paris and Switzerland. I had not seen my dad's family since I was three years old. Learning about the culture in which my dad grew up made me realize that I had taken many things for granted, from his personality quirks to his cooking skills. I learned a great deal from my dad, and while spending time with his brothers and my grandmother (his mother), I saw him smile again. Dad finally began to make sense to me, even if it was only in this small window of time. I realized how easily one's personal choice, such as a bad marriage, could lead to misfortune that alters one's life.

Years later, I announced to my Dad that I was engaged and getting married to the man I loved. Still hurting from his broken marriage, Dad mumbled, "Love, ha, I am in no position to give any marital advice." During the wedding reception he was very uncomfortable being seated next to my mother, and being asked to smile as the cameras flashed.

My husband and I decided to live close to my mother. This was not my choice, but he genuinely felt sorry for her. We helped in the housecleaning and invited her to share our meals. Living nearby provided a source of healing and I found her to be a great asset when she became a grandmother. Although her mental illness was debilitating, for the most part she was very supportive of me and I began to appreciate her more.

I validate many of my father's concerns when he faced divorce. But all was not healed when my mother was removed from the family. Years following, I had to learn how to deal with human relationships outside of the Buchmann "Crisis Management" years. Trust and intimacy were difficult to master, and I had to overcome the struggle of selfishness.

I have a strong empathy for my father's suffering. As the oldest, I think I can relate best to the family hardships; my brothers don't have the same recollection as I do of living with a mentally ill mother and a father in desperation. God gave me two parents, one with a mental illness and one without. It hurt me deeply that during my teenage years I felt the absence from both. My father's survival strategy and his parenting style did not help me then. I do, however, recognize my dad's effort in the years that followed. When my kids were born, he was always the first visitor in the hospital, even if it was past midnight. He sees great hope in the next Buchmann generation.

COULD I HAVE DONE BETTER?

Each time I read the stories of my children again, I relive the calamity and ask, "Could I have done better? Did I do my best under the circumstances?" I empathize with Holly and thank her for the patience of looking after the four younger brothers so well. Perry is right by saying that our home ran like a business without a human resources department. Yes, we were understaffed. A nanny cannot replace a mother, nor can a father play both roles. Although the younger boys did better because they entered the teenage years when the home life began to normalize, they had to get tough and stand their ground, defending the bullying of the older siblings. Sorry, boys.

The years leading to Sophie's departure were most trying and the children have good reason to be critical of their mother and me. As a single dad I wasn't able to provide the same time and devotion to each child that a two-parent family could. I don't blame them a bit for how they feel. I am an entrepreneur who has little patience and downplayed grievances that appeared petty. My time for each child was measured, and I only attended to pressing issues. Survival and getting results was my main objective. Affection took second place.

No, our home wasn't a perfect model by any stretch of the imagination and the children had to raise themselves. This is consistent with large families of past generations, which also reminds me of my own upbringing on the busy farm back home. My father made us believe it was a matter of survival, and perhaps it was. We all had to chip in. The farm produce fed the family and the wood collected from the trees served as fuel to cook and heat the house. There were no thermostats to control the room temperature, nor did we have a car to pick up groceries from a convenient supermarket. We were mostly self-sufficient.

If I could do it again, I would reach out more to the two oldest children, even though they didn't ask for it. They pretended they knew it all, and I only learned later that they hurt the most. The younger ones got more from me because they listened, were easier to please, appreciated my efforts, and caused less trouble than the older ones.

My children mention that I was an absent father and, yes, I was often away. The work demanded long hours and some travel, essentials to building a company. Working away from home was good for me in that it diverted my attention from the nagging family problems. I may have chosen more of this than was absolutely necessary when Sophie was still living at home. I needed an escape from the continuous pandemonium of the deteriorating marriage. My task was to get through another day, head up, and coping with the many challenges that arose inside and outside the home.

I wanted to be a good father, but the marital tension leading up to the separation, and then dealing with the complex legal issues during the three-year divorce proceedings, drained much of my energy and robbed me of the day-to-day care that should have gone to the children. Some level of child neglect cannot be avoided if a family lies in ruins and needs rebuilding. I tried to catch up with quality time by cooking good meals and reading bedtime stories, but I was often too tired and wanted to become invisible, slip into my bedroom, close the door, and get some quiet time for myself.

Children know that parents are human beings who occasionally mess up, have limitations in endurance, and need time to relax. Youngsters are far more resilient than many folks might think. The occasional slippage is less damaging than having a stable home, backed by parental leadership that is solid, loving, and fair. They want a mom and dad who can be trusted, have good morals, and are leading by a example. Most of all, children want someone who is consistent and mentally stable.

Report Card on My Parenting

During a recent family retreat at a Whistler resort, I asked the now grown children to judge my handling of the family crisis. I soon realized that the hurt of the past is still deeply entrenched in their hearts. I had hoped that the passing of time would have erased these dark memories. This hasn't happened yet and, in part, they blame me for the rough ride. Pointing the finger at a parent is common. I pointed a finger also during my growing-up years.

I left the old country without resolving the issues that troubled me most. It would have helped if my father had explained the circumstances that led to what I thought was unfair punishment. Admitting shortcomings and letting me know that no parent is perfect would have drawn me closer to Dad. Insisting on being right when the child thinks otherwise casts a dark shadow on the parent-child relationship. A father may think he is doing well, but the child sees the theatrical play from a different angle.

We all have an axe to grind and remember unpleasant incidents that happened while growing up. These memories become the "wailing wall" to which we flee to release our grief. Everyone remembers unfairness—some small, others large, some justified, others not. We preserve them in our memory as if they were valuable treasures, and bring them into adulthood so that we can replay them again. Each time we recall an incident we add drama, and what goes back into memory is an enhanced adaptation that overwrites the original version.

I detect some embellishments with my own children. As the saying goes, "Children are the world's greatest recorders but the world's worst interpreters." As parents we try to downplay irregularities that upset our children and focus on the *finish line* instead. We look at the skirmishes and mishaps as unfortunate incidents that couldn't be avoided and deem ourselves successful when the children turn out well and lead productive lives.

My family expresses emotions best by e-mail. Among a flurry of messages, Holly articulated her thoughts by saying, "You write as though your role was absolutely faultless. You don't humble yourself, nor do you admit to your mistakes. They are always justified with a fleeting reason. What if you had been more in tune with Mom's emotional needs right from the beginning and sought to fight the illness together?" She then stated that I am always trying to rationalize my actions, including the divorce.

Holly was supportive of the divorce but questions my approach. She has also criticized that I wasn't always emotionally available to her, Perry, and the other children. When her mother hurt her during a family dispute, the 911 call she made was a cry of desperation. It was an urgent attempt to thrust open the door so an outsider could see what was happening inside. She was shouting for help.

Perry writes that the divorce was necessary for the kids because it was the lesser of the two evils. He stated, however, that, "Dad chose to focus on his company and not engage in our lives. He was too much in a survival mode and didn't provide enough emotional support."

The younger three boys give more credit for my parenting role. Mattie, the middle child who had gone through a great deal of hurt growing up, wrote that he had no regrets in the way he had been raised and thinks that the type of upbringing motivates him to attain more in life. He says that, although not perfect, the rearing strangely worked.

Todd, who was in early grade school during the family crisis, explained that the lack of parental supervision made him more mature and independent. "Let's keep in mind that we were raised during a crisis time," he says. "No one had it easy, especially Dad. It's unfair to expect Dad to be the full-time father and mother of five growing kids. Given the circumstances, I understand why Dad raised us this way. We expected too much from him."

Somewhat sheltered from the storm, Randy, our youngest, sent me this moving message: "Dad, I think it is a miracle that somehow you raised five kids while going through a roller-coaster marriage and running a business. You did the best job possible and I am not at all bitter about the way I grew up. For the most part, the house was stable and always welcoming."

In the midst of the floods of criticisms, a surprising incident happened just recently. Randy came home from work and said that his boss gave him a compliment: "Go home and tell your dad that he has brought you up very well, and thank him for it." Puzzled by this comment made by a total stranger, I thought that God has a way of stepping in to defend the accused in times of trial.

My broken marriage has made my children cautious of getting married. They worry that their loving dates could turn into monsters one day. The boys keep asking, "Dad, were there any signs of problems when you married Mom?" To which I reply, "No, *none*." I then advise them to go ahead and marry the person they love. I emphasize that with goodwill and prayer most marriages work out well. Very few must be dissolved. Having tasted the bitter pill of a failed marriage I understand their concerns and pray that my divorce will serve as a sacrificial offering so that my children will be spared this horrible ordeal.

Holly, her husband, and their small children moved back to live in our family home. This will enable her husband to complete his nursing studies. To make it comfortable for them, we installed a kitchen so they have their own living quarters. Dwelling under one roof brings us closer together again, and I am able to make up for my role as father. I also realize how much fun grandchildren are. We share the piano, and I must keep up with my playing or else the talented next generation will put me to shame. This grand piano has been a great blessing for our family. It provides fun and enjoyment for everyone.

In her concluding e-mail Holly writes, "You shouldn't feel guilt whatsoever. In every way, you have exceeded as a father and grandfather. I have accepted that times were rough and your empathy was a healing medicine to me." The boys added these words, "You led by the example of being unselfish, using a strong moral and ethical code, being consistent in advice and punishment, and never choosing favorites."

What Counselors Say

As parent and breadwinner, my duty was (and still is) to create a stable home by setting firm rules, and then go out and earn a living. This wasn't possible when Sophie was still living at home. She acted as a lightning rod for the children, undermining my authority, and letting them get away with murder. I was aware of the flaw and knew that one pillar supporting the family structure was caving in, causing the building to list to one side. The children took advantage of this and gravitated to the path of least resistance. Allowing this to continue would have caused an eventual collapse. Sophie's departure prevented it from happening and the family regained equilibrium, albeit on only one pillar.

Many families suffer from serious deficiencies and Christian counselors, broadcasters, and authors of self-help books are eager to assist by offering tons of resource material. Although well-meaning, the information often fails to address the more serious family problems, especially if it involves a dysfunctional partner.

I detect a trace of ignorance with these self-help resources in that the advisors prefer taking a home setting in which two functioning parents is the norm. They assume that the family's crisis would be resolved if proper guidelines were given and followed. In short, advisors pick cases where the offered resources would have a positive impact to remedy the situation.

A family dysfunction that can only be resolved with a divorce is a taboo. It's something that's not supposed to happen, and Christian advisors stay away from this alternative. Very few would suggest divorce, even if this were the best solution. Simply saying that "Our hands are bound by the Bible," as some ministers do, is not a good answer when a hurting family falls apart because it can no longer function under the repressive scheme of an irrational spouse. Books and programs do indeed help if the problems are mild and correctable, but giving advice on *interior decoration* is inappropriate if the house is collapsing.

"What did you go out into the desert to see?" Jesus asked the folks who visited John the Baptist. "A reed swayed by the wind? If not, what did you go out to see? A man dressed in fine clothes? No, those who wear fine clothes are in kings' palaces."

These words from Matthew 11:7–8 remind us of the harsh environment in a desert, and the unfamiliarity when sheltered people visited the wasteland. Applying this biblical verse to modern marriage and family counseling, advisers must come to grips with the harsh reality when helping a dysfunctional family. Not all spouses are blessed with a healthy and rational mind. Many are simply not able, or willing, to follow outside advice when given. The textbook approach, even if Christian based, has limited benefit if the old house needs rebuilding.

"A parent should always engage fully in the children's lives," is a common phrase I hear from well-meaning advisors. How can a single parent do this when he or she is also the sole breadwinner? As my finances got tighter and the legal bills kept rising, my divorce lawyer

hinted that I might have to pull the children out of Christian education, sell the house, and find a place to rent. I didn't follow her advice
and instead moved the financial urgency to a higher priority by putting
in extra hours at work. Working hard is not always done for material
enrichment and self-fulfillment, as some well-meaning advisors might
believe. For many it's survival!

When soft advice no longer provides a solid underpinning to rebuild
your family, then you, the responsible parent, must take a leadership
position and go on your own. Let's not forget that help is available from
above for those who ask. "I will never leave you, nor forsake you . . . The
Lord is my helper and I will not fear," says the Bible.

This verse from Hebrews 13:5,6 became true and our family survived the crisis. I was pleased when Todd told me how proud he is that
I started Cadex and appreciates that I am able to pay the tuition for his
study at UBC to become an engineer.

We must accept that many parents are called to do more than raise
children. Our forefathers worked hard to provide the freedom and
prosperity that we take for granted today. They did this above their
parental responsibility, and many went through deep hardship. While
textbook counsel will work for some, Blaise Pascal[14] reminds us: "The
supreme function of reason is to show man that some things are beyond
reason."

RESTITUTION

The bullying incident mentioned in Mattie's story continued to bother
me and I wanted closure. There is evidence that children who had been
physically abused want to pass on their inner feelings to others in form
of bullying. A study by York University psychologist Dr. Debra Pepler
concludes that children who bully often lack "a moral compass" and
"experience a great deal of conflict in their relationships with their
parents."[a] Psychologists say further that the spirit of a bully is broken.
He or she has low tolerance, lacks self-esteem, is frustrated, and wants
to get even by hitting someone of lesser stature who is unlikely to fight
back. The stocky, blond, blue-eyed boy whom Mattie bullied was such

a person. We tried contacting him and asking for forgiveness, but he had moved away and could no longer be reached.

We then focused on an equally troubling incident that came to light when the boys exchanged their foolish pranks as part of the story writing. I learned that Mattie had embezzled money from a classmate in grade school. Shawn came from an immigrant family and was new in class. Mattie demanded money and threatened him with physical punishment if he didn't comply. Shy and intimidated, Shawn gave in and gradually delivered the cash, amounting to several hundred dollars over time. I assume that the funds were stolen from his parents' household provisions.

Even though twelve years have passed since the event happened, I wanted Mattie to confess and return the money. The exercise would teach him a lesson for an offense he committed in the past. This was especially important because he was not caught and there was no punishment.

The school assisted me in locating Shawn's new address and phone number. I dialed the number and his mother answered. I explained briefly what had happened and then asked to speak to her son. When Shawn picked up the receiver and heard the story, he was moved with emotion. He indicated that returning the money would be wonderful.

Over the weekend we collected the funds. Most came from Mattie. His younger brother, Todd, also chipped in and I gave the rest. Then we hopped on our bicycles and headed down to New Westminster, where Shawn lives. I waited in the front yard of the house while Mattie went to the door and rang the bell. It wasn't long before Shawn opened the door.

Mattie and Shawn looked tense at first, but when Mattie handed over the envelope containing the money and a friendship card, both were overtaken with emotion. The two lads had not seen each other since the grade school days. They began exchanging memories, each wanting to know how the other was doing. Both young men were moved with an inner joy because something positive had come from a wrongful act. Mattie then asked Shawn for forgiveness and the two lads departed as good friends. The rain shower that began falling on our way home served as a cleansing act to wash our hearts clean.

Christians who divorce are torn between strict church rules and the forbidden exit. Rejected, confused, and entangled in a mire of religious dogma with little spiritual support, many seek refuge in the secular world and find comfort there.

CHAPTER 14

POWER OF PRAYERS

GOD'S PROVIDENCE OVER MY FAMILY

I have witnessed God's protection over my life and the family in amazing ways. Looking back, I cannot stop marveling at the wonderful support our Good Lord has given us. His invisible hand guided us through many treacherous canyons. We survived, and for lack of any other explanation, I call these mishaps miracles. Such a miracle occurred when I was a teenager. It was a mishap that almost cost me my life.

During a summer vacation I wanted to experience the Mediterranean Sea and drove my 50cc moped to Marseille. Arriving at this big French city after two days of travel, the sea spread out in an incredible display of beauty against the blue sky. It was a hot day and I decided to cool off by stepping into the refreshing waters. Not able to swim, I kept to the shallow shoreline by wading the rocky beach on the west side of the city. Gradually I went a bit deeper, cooling off and enjoying the brilliant sunshine above. Then, suddenly, the ground gave way and I couldn't touch bottom anymore. Thrashing about wildly, I was swept under the water. I was drowning! My last thought was, "This is it," and passed out.

I woke up on the beach. I had been pulled a safe distance from the water. A group of rough-looking beach kids stared down at me, speaking in an unfamiliar language. Feeling embarrassed, I stood up, picked up my clothes, hopped on my moped and headed back to the city as if nothing had happened. I didn't want to associate myself with this mob. They made feel me uncomfortable. I didn't understand all this staring and fussing over me. As I sped off they yelled unintelligible words at me, but I couldn't understand them.

It only dawned on me later that I had drowned and was unconscious. I remembered slipping on the rock, going down, and passing out. I asked, *how long was I unconscious, and how did I make it to safety?* One of these beach kids must have seen me go down, jumped into the water, and pulled me out. Without his heroic act I would not have survived. I simply woke up on that beach as if I had slept, and had no side effects. I never thanked anyone, and I hope that God has rewarded the person for the bravery in saving my life.

Each of my children's births was a miracle. The birth of Holly, our firstborn, was especially difficult. After Sophie's 24 hours in labor with no progress, the nurse finally wheeled my wife into the birthing room. I was allowed in at first, but when the problems persisted the doctor kicked me out. I must have asked silly questions that triggered the discharge.

Waiting outside was agonizing. I paced up and down the hallway, not knowing what was going on behind closed doors. Then I heard a page on the PA system, urgently calling for a pediatrician. Within a short time a doctor came and hurried inside. Not long afterward, another call sounded over the intercom. This was for a specialist. A doctor hurried toward the birthing room and entered. "What is going on?" I asked a doctor who was just leaving the room. Not paying any attention to me, he skirted away without answering and disappeared down the long hallway.

Frantic with worry, I began praying The Lord's Prayer very slowly and intensely, meditating on each verse, starting with "Our Father, who art in heaven." When I came to the last verse, which says, ". . . and lead us not into temptation," I heard the cry of a baby. My daughter had been born! Immediately, the door flung wide open and I was welcomed in to meet the cutest baby on earth. What a comfort to see my smiling wife, the relieved faces of the doctors, and the happy nurses. Each subsequent birth was a miracle of same dimension that no one can fully comprehend.

I remember when Mattie, a toddler, escaped the house on his pedal car and drove down the street, passed through the intersection, and headed toward a dead end at the bottom of the hill. Running after him, I was able to catch up and stop him. When he was a bit older, this same boy was run over by a truck on his way home from kindergarten. He followed his older brother at a busy intersection, and trying to catch up he began crossing the street when the light changed. The truck driver couldn't see the little boy over the tall motor hood and Mattie was thrown onto the pavement. There he was, lying in the middle of the street beneath a heavy truck and bleeding from his head! By God's grace, the wheels didn't run over him. He only received a wound when the muffler grazed the back of his head. Luckily, the injury was not serious.

While traveling in the San Francisco Bay Area, Mattie, then in early grade school, became very ill, and I carried him into a doctor's office. The physician prescribed medication and told us to go to the emergency room right away. While my wife was getting the medicine at a nearby shopping mall, I sat with Mattie in the minivan. There he was, still and pale, complaining of nausea. Feeling helpless, I stepped outside and began walking around the vehicle, praying for my son's healing. With each turn I observed Mattie's slumped-down head, and there was no improvement. After about the seventh circle and while still praying, Mattie sudden looked up at me and asked a question about money, his favorite topic. His face showed color and he looked alert. Amazed, I asked, "Are you feeling better?"

"Yes, Dad," he said, "I'm fine now." And indeed, he was better.

No one knows what happened in that hot parking lot. When my wife came back with the medication, Mattie no longer showed any symptoms of the illness. We felt so confident about the healing that we headed straight home to Vancouver—a two-day drive. We never visited the emergency room, and Mattie was well.

Just recently I quizzed him about the miraculous recovery. He is now in his mid-twenties and has a lot going for him. "Yes, I remember how sick I was," he said, and described ". . . all of the sudden I felt well. It was as if a heavy burden had lifted." He tried to explain but couldn't give a reason why he was well so quickly. I told him that I had been praying for healing and that I believe in miracles.

At 16 years of age my boys wanted to drive. With the financial help of their mother (against my will), they bought fast cars and big motorcycles. My oldest son, Perry, was the first to get into these racing machines. He participated in many competitions and was soon rated in the top five percent of his racing club. His activities, however, began to worry me. He and Mattie bragged about hair-raising incidents that had caused serious injury to participants. Even though their machines did crash, the boys escaped serious injury as if protected by an invisible hand.

That invisible hand was also present the night Mattie took his newly acquired Porsche for a spin. He spent the whole day polishing the exterior and treating the leather seats of this second-hand car. It was raining that night, and not being familiar with excessive power on the back wheels, he spun out of control on a curve and wrapped the car around an electrical pole. The vehicle was so badly mangled that the emergency crew had to use the Jaws of Life to get him out of the wreckage. Again, he escaped serious injury.

Mattie wanted to go for one final round on the motorcycle race-track in Spokane, Washington, before heading home. Perhaps he was tired from earlier races that day and should have called it quits. This last round could have cost his life. He lost control at full speed and crashed. The heavy motorbike catapulted through the air and bounced off the ground several times before coming to rest. Again, by God's grace, Mattie escaped major injury. Another time, Mattie lost muscle strength while swimming in a lake in the rugged wilderness of British Columbia, and his friend had to rescue him. God must have appointed this young man to watch over Mattie and be there at the right time.

From early childhood to young adulthood, armies of guardian angels have worked overtime to protect my children. I believe in the power of prayer and in God's divine help. It is comforting to know that there is someone higher up who watches over us. There is a God who knows our struggles and brings us to safety when we are lost and in peril. To express doubts about a supernatural spirit is human, but to deny the existence of an Almighty God touches on ignorance. St. Thomas Aquinas (1225-1274) said:

> To one with faith, no explanation is needed, to one without faith, no explanation is possible.
>
> —St. Thomas Aquinas

UNFULFILLED DREAMS

When we marry and start a family, we carry with us the hope for a better world. We glance at the generation that has passed before us, see their failings, and resolve to do better. God appreciates our noble intentions but also places obstacles in our journey.

Life can be portrayed as hewing a path through dense bush, not knowing where we are heading and not understanding what lies ahead in the untouched wilderness. Every morning, replenished with fresh energy, we grab the axe and advance further into unfamiliar territory.

Then, when autumn comes, our strikes get slower but more skilled and calculated. We stop for breath, look back at the hewn path, and reminisce about the past. It's then that we see the carnage strewn along the way and wonder if we could have done better.

One piece of carnage on the trail is my broken marriage. It is a bloodshed that cannot be flushed out. I am reminded of this each time I attend a family event to which my "ex" is also invited. Yes, we do meet occasionally and the connection can never be broken. Reality cannot be changed, nor can it be erased.

I feel awkward in her presence. We greet each other and keep our distance. Looking at her now, I can hardly believe that this perplexed and estranged woman was once the loving young lady God chose to be my wife. I simply have no answer as to what God had in mind—giving in marriage and taking away in divorce—if one can put God into the equation. *I must have taken a wrong turn while hacking away the dense brush*, I reckon. *Or was this my destiny, a carefully thought-out plan, orchestrated by Someone higher*, I ask? I will never know.

Medicine has made wonderful progress but none so effective that would allow Sophie to lead a normal life. Now in her fifties, she looks happy and seems satisfied with her life, but she has to be reminded to get more exercise, watch what she eats, and observe personal hygiene. In conversations with her, one realizes that much of what she says is fantasy. One cannot take what she says for real. Her days revolve around living in a cramped apartment that she manages herself, calling her children by phone, looking forward to visits by the children on weekends, and accepting invitations for family celebrations.

There are times when she gets depressed, and my children make a special effort to lift her up. The long winter months are especially hard on her. When down she stops taking her medication, begins having anxiety attacks, and becomes afraid to leave her apartment. She tells wild stories, misplaces articles, becomes irritable, and gets paranoid about food spoilage if a food item has been left out of the refrigerator for even a few minutes.

My children are doing a fine job attending to her needs. But what is my duty? How should I relate to my former wife? The Bible doesn't address the do's and don'ts of ex-spouses, but reminds us to look after the sick, helpless, and poor. "Love your neighbor as you love yourself," says Jesus, and reminds us, "What you do for the least of these, you do for me."

Not everyone is blessed with a healthy and rational mind, and if divorce is necessary, the former spouse should continue supporting the "ex" outside of marriage. This sends a strong message to the children to care for the needy. Sophie would have done everything in her power to escape the debilitating bipolar disease.

I've tried to help and be tolerant, but I get cranky when I come home from work and find her puttering around my house. It's hard to love an ex-spouse after a difficult marriage. Even after all these years, something deep inside my chest keeps churning. It's an irritant I can never fully remove, even though I have forgiven Sophie.

My "ex" is very kind to me now. She means well and is the first to greet me with good wishes on Christmas, New Year, and my birthday. The resentment that had built up during our troubled marriage and the lengthy divorce proceedings has turned to acceptance and silent respect. I admire her as the mother of my children and appreciate the sacrifices she has made in giving me five healthy offspring, a gift that can never be overlooked.

I am still single. Remarriage would be nice but there is fear of getting into another difficult relationship. The experience of my previous marriage can never be fully expunged. The risk is simply too great. I cannot help but look at marriage as if it were a screen door. Flies that are on the outside want to get in, and those trapped inside want to get out.

I realize that being married has definite advantages. Divorce carries a stigma of failure that only a loving new spouse and a happy new union could remove.

I have dated a few ladies, but none have led to a lasting relationship. Ending a new friendship after much hope and anticipation causes nothing but grief and disappointment for both parties. I am also concerned that a new union could cause havoc within my family. We are doing well now, and a change could upset our stable nucleus.

The boys accepted my desire to find a new partner but weren't enthusiastic about the dating part. Each time my date visited the house the boys had something negative to say about her. The mind of youngsters is razor sharp and I took their comments seriously. This made me cautious, and I finally decided to put my lady friend to a test in an unconventional way. She lived a sheltered life and was a bit shy. I wanted to see if she could cope with my rowdy teenagers. So I took her for a long walk, and while enjoying the countryside, I posed this question to her, "What would you say if one of my teenagers said, 'I hate you?'"

There was silence. I wasn't sure if she had heard the question and I was ready to repeat it. Then, finally, she spoke up and said in a soft voice that was barely audible, "Take me home!"

The question was too harsh for her. It struck like lightning. She was shocked and disgusted that I would ask her this. Her face looked paler than normal and had no expression. During the drive back, she didn't speak a word and didn't accept my diner invitation. I explained to her later the reason for my asking, but she thought the question was too farfetched. Being devoted Christians, we prayed for direction, and this led to me to discontinue the relationship.

Prayer may not necessarily solve a problem, but it enlightens the path. Had she been prepared to stand up to the challenges, she would have said something like this to the youngsters, "Yes, I understand how you feel about me, but I love you and want to help you. Tell me how I can do this." She had never been married, had no children, and was not familiar with the bumps and bruises a parent gets in raising children. She only knew "virtual parenting," an environment that is far from reality.

Did the children see beyond my desire to marry? Did they perceive the date as an intruder who could upset our family? Yes, I believe they did. They wanted my full and undivided attention, and feared that a third party would upset the harmony. This became evident during dinner invitations, when I tried to please my lady friend and the children. Instead of becoming a unified party, two opposing camps formed, neither of which could be satisfied. The children left the dinner table as soon as they could. This reminded me of the visit to Switzerland when my loyalty was split between Sophie and my mother. I tried pleasing both parties, but could not. Matthew 6:24 says, "No one can serve two masters. Either he will hate the one and love the other, or he will be devoted to the one and despise the other."

I believe that the welfare of the children must come before personal desires, even if this means postponing remarriage or remaining single. Many single parents do well raising the family by themselves. A second marriage might work if the custodian cannot cope with the family obligations and the new partner would stabilize the home. Remarriage looks attractive indeed, but a blended family opens new challenges.

Should I pray for a suitable partner again? I ask. This brings me back to my childhood when I prayed 4,000 Hail Marys. I also recall going to church to remind God of my long wish list but got caught by the priest. "Would a second marriage work out better?" I ask. I realize that we cannot blame God for our misfortune. I do hope, however, that the Good Lord will one day restore something I value so much—namely marriage. After all, God restored the marriage of Job and they lived happily ever after.

Although my life is jam-packed with running a busy household, managing my company, and writing this book, I know that one day my children will move out and I will be left alone in the house. What will I do when the waiting at the railroad crossing is over and the last train car disappears in the dusk down the track? Will I stare at the many family photos and fix the marks on the walls that the kids left behind? Will I finally find the free time for myself that I have always wanted? Or will I just be lonely? Perhaps this will be the time to consider remarriage.

We all have unfulfilled dreams. God gives and God takes away. In my quest for answers I have come to realize that the Lord has provided me with much more than I asked for. My family is functional again. The children are healthy and we are doing well. The squandered money has been redeemed many times over. Most importantly, the Lord has shown me how to enjoy the simple things of life. They are gifts that have no price. Looking around me I see miracle upon miracle—marvels hidden from those who only seek material riches, fame, and worldly pleasures. I witness the splendor of nature that renews itself in a most miraculous way. In Psalm 19:1–4 we read:

> The heavens are telling the glory of God; they are a marvelous display of His craftsmanship. Day and night they keep on telling about God. Without a sound or word, silent in the skies, their message reaches out to all the world.
>
> —TLB

You may carry a heavy load and travel on a road that is laborious, long, and seemingly leading to nowhere. If you have unfulfilled dreams and are bogged down with persistent marital problems, I suggest the following:

- Try to stop the transgression. Remove yourself from the onslaught of the hurts and arguments by getting time and space for yourself. This will allow you to reflect on available options.

- Pray in quiet and ask God for a solution. Involve your relatives and close friends and ask them to pray also. Do not give up if it takes longer than expected.
- Forgive the person who causes affliction. Healing can only begin once you have opened your heart and forgiven the oppressor. If you cannot forgive, pray for the person. This will set you free.
- Attend regular church services. Quiet meditation away from home builds strength and gives wisdom. Worshiping with others will expand your understanding beyond the walls of the home and bring you into a supporting community.

During my darkest days, Frank and Mary, my longtime supporting friends, gave me a famous poem in a beautiful frame, entitled, "Footsteps in the Sand." It describes a walk with the Lord on a beach. First, we see two sets of footprints in the sand, but when times get tough, there is only one. After asking the Lord why He would leave me when I needed Him most, He replied, "It was then that I carried you."[a]

Looking back, God's help was most prevalent when I was down and out, and the path was obscured. I was never alone and help was always available. It is most striking that God sent His help through ordinary people.

GOD WORKS FOR THE GOOD OF THOSE WHO LOVE HIM

In closing, let us examine Romans 8:28 once more. It says, "And we know that in all things God works for the good of those who love him, who have been called according to his purpose." In view of my broken marriage I have struggled with this verse for a long time. "God working for the good in all things" troubles me when I consider the encroaching illness of my wife that tore our family apart. I also question the text when I hear about accidents, fires, tornados, earthquakes, and tsunamis that kill innocent people. I have a hard time seeing anything as "working for our good" when widows long for their deceased spouses and orphans cry out for their mothers and fathers who will never return.

Romans 8:28 has been the subject of much commentary. Biblical scholars say that we must read the verse in the context of a broader text that stretches from Romans 8:14 to 8:39. By reading the entire passage, we begin seeing a different picture. God allows these awful things to happen, but promises never to abandon us because nothing can separate us from the love of God. He provides us with steadfastness regardless of what must come to pass. The key is not so much on how floods, earthquakes, and hurricanes supposedly "work for our good," but on how these terrible things do not restrict God in bringing good out of the ashes. Let these calamities be what they are, acts of God over which we have little control. We have no clear answers as to why they happen, other than pointing to the laws of physics. As long as our planet keeps spinning around its axis and the sun rises above our heads, disasters will occur.

Accepting and enduring calamities, even if we don't understand why they happen, brings us into a higher realm of the spiritual world. Good things came from my broken marriage. I am a richer person in spirit for one, and I would not have written this book if I had not experienced adversity. Dr. James Dobson[5] writes, "Those who conquer their problems are more secure than those who never face them." In this respect, conquering is better than not conquering, and there is truth in Romans 8:28. Hardship builds spiritual understanding, insight that cannot be obtained from academia.

The apostle Paul said good-bye to us with a sense of satisfaction and accomplishment. He was a man who had achieved great things in his life even while enduring many adversities. What amazes me is how well he took hardship. In 2 Timothy 4:7 we read: "I have fought the good fight, I have finished the race, I have kept the faith." The punch line is *"I have kept the faith."*

No, God didn't respond to my prayers in the way I wanted. I despised divorce with a passion because it broke the promise I had made. I hoped for a miracle through which God would reveal His awesome power and provide healing similar to the awakening of Lazarus from the grave. It did not happen. Instead, I (the very person who despised divorce as a self-inflicted act) had to stoop down low and go through this humiliating experience. I thought I was invincible, and in my haughty spirit, I believed that commitment to marriage and following biblical principles would solve all ills. I stood on dry ground and from my vantage point looked down into the abyss of divorce. I criticized those who, in my limited understanding, didn't do so well with their marriages. This club mentality blinded me from seeing the real reasons why some marriages cannot survive and why it is better to resolve them.

I believe in the power of prayer and I am convinced that the restoration of my family, the success of my business, my good health, and the return of inner happiness are God's answers to prayer. I couldn't have done it by myself. Our marriage was successful in that it served as the vehicle to deliver the goods—five children. The chicks are hatched, the product is delivered, but the eggshells lie broken on the floor.

With the children growing into young adults I asked the question, "What's more important, the marriage or the family; the eggshells or the content?" We know that both are needed, but if only one could be chosen, I would take the family. The family forms a new generation that holds the aspirations I cherish, namely *to set forth faithful soldiers who carry the good deed by walking in the footprints of the Lord.*

God mandated a marriage to be permanent. He did this for good reason—to instill discipline and order to the human race. It's a very good plan that works most of the time, but there are exceptions. God knows about these and allows them to happen.

It wasn't so much the divorce that caused my spiritual free-fall, but the thought that God had neglected me on something I treasured so much. Not getting help from above at a critical moment was a huge letdown. I felt as if God had abandoned me in the trenches for good. But looking back, this very walk in the dumps changed my life for the better.

Can we attain prominence without enduring hardship? No, we must go through disappointments in life to gain strength and reach greatness in spirit. "Rejoicing in suffering," as the apostle Paul says in Romans 5:3–4, does not make much sense when we are victims of uncontrolled circumstances and are being tossed in a merciless sea. It was during the betrayal barrier that I gained a new understanding that true happiness does not lie in *achieving*, but in *surrendering and accepting*. We must become servants of the Lord by letting go of our own desires and following Him. The yoke He prepared for me was easier to bear than I had first anticipated.

170

It's not the journey that counts, but the arrival. A stream of water is born on top of the mountain. It endures many twists, twirls, and torrents until it meets the big master and finds a home in the mighty ocean. God pays little attention to what *role* we play on the theatrical stage, but observes *how* we play our part.

In closing we reflect on the well-known prayer by Rev. Dr. Reinhold Niebuhr[13.] It reminds us of the immeasurable gift that God gives to most of us—it's the heritage of a healthy mind. I beg that we use this powerful tool for the benefit of our families and the good of the society at large, and pray:

> God grant me the SERENITY to accept the things I cannot change, COURAGE to change the things I can, and the WISDOM to know the difference. Living one day at a time, enjoying one moment at a time, accepting hardships and the pathway of peace, and trusting that God will make all things right.
>
> —Rev. Dr. Reinhold Niebuhr

WITH SPECIAL THANKS

I want to take the opportunity to thank those who have contributed to this book. First in line are my five children, who supported me throughout my writing. They gave me valuable suggestions of what can be said and what should be kept private. Writing their own stories conveys a strong desire to share the experience with others. Special appreciation goes to Holly for reading through several editions and catching errors others had missed.

The material would not be as articulate and far-reaching had it not been for the tireless contributions of devout church leaders and lay people from both Catholic and Protestant denominations. These faithful believers took it on themselves to read the draft copies and provide an honest opinion. Most agree with the content and accept that *divorce for just cause* is poorly understood, especially in church communities. They assisted me in formulating critical sentences, allowing me to be explicit, articulate, and frank, and yet biblically correct and inoffensive to believers.

I honor the desire not to mention names. The suggestions made are strictly "off the record"; a voice from the wilderness, so to say. Names are less important than the message carried and the ability to help the less fortunate in marriage. Thank you, voices without names from the wilderness, for having been so open and forthright with me.

EPILOGUE

The Buchmann clan is doing well. The oldest three children are happily married with children of their own, and more weddings will be in the planning. Although the divorce made them skeptical about religion and, for a while, withdrew from going to church, all are regular churchgoers again. Providing silent leadership by attending church services myself is the best formula to entice others to follow suit.

All my children are successful in their careers. Holly does what is most important of all, raising three beautiful children. Perry has become a strong business leader, and Mattie is good in sales and human relations. Todd has earned his civil engineering degree at UBC and is playing American football in Switzerland during the summer of 2009. The organizers chose him for his superior playing skills. Randy is finishing his postgraduate education and, being the youngest, he reminds me of biblical David, who was courageous, well liked, and became a great leader. Robert has these same qualities.

After more medical treatments, Sophie is stable and content most of the time. With the help of care workers visiting her three times a day, she manages her own apartment. My children visit her often and we meet at family gatherings. Her mental health is fragile and she suffers depression if one of her children travels or does not call at the appointed time. She is especially fond of the youngest two boys and does not associate much with her sisters living close by.

Remarriage and loving a spouse again would have been one of my highest callings in life, but I remain single. I cannot escape the fear of failing to meet the desires of a new spouse and being chastised again. The experience of my last marriage is still vivid in my mind. I enjoy my freedom, and with Randy still living at home, we get away with things that we couldn't do if we had a woman in the house. It's nice to have Randy around; he is an excellent cook and comes up with new cooking experiments.

While sitting at the deathbed of my mother I was reminded again of the 4,000 Hail Marys I prayed as a small boy. At nearly 92, she still sold fruits and vegetables at the family farm in Switzerland the week before. I happened to be in Europe on business when I heard that she had been admitted to the hospital but was told she was doing better. Nevertheless, I made last-minute flight changes to be with her.

My mother was surprised to see me that morning. She was feeling better and the hospital had made arrangements for her to go home. As it turned out, the home-going was to a different place. We gently stroked her body, tearfully saying good-bye, as she passed away that afternoon.

There was great sadness for the loss of a dear mother; and at the same time there was joy for having lived a good and productive life. She never wanted to live in a seniors' home but be useful to humanity to the very end. My mother was well prepared to go, and the Hail Marys delivered the promise. The last verse of the prayer carries a message we all long for—someone to pray for us to grant a graceful departure. I beg that this heavenly grace will also be with me at the end of my pilgrimage on earth, when I am being called home.

REFERENCE NAMES

1. **St. Teresa of Avila** (1515–1582), baptized as Teresa de Cepeda y Ahumada, was born to a well-to-do family in Spain and later entered the Carmelite Order. Her mother died when she was 15, leaving behind ten children. Teresa was beautiful and had good social skills, but was in poor health and endured much suffering.

2. **Catechism** is a system of Christian teaching used in the Jewish synagogues and adapted by the early Christian churches. After neglect, the great Roman Catholic Council of Trent (1563) redis-covered the value of the catechism.

3. **Chuck Colson** (Charles Wendell Colson) gave up his lucrative law practice in New York to become the chief counsel for President Richard Nixon. He was imprisoned for Watergate-related charges. After his early release, he founded Prison Fellowship, a Christian nonprofit organization that assists prisoners and ex-prisoners. Colson is a famous public speaker and the author of many books.

4. **Dr. Charles A. Cummins** is a retired school administrator, former mathematics teacher, and author of the weekly newspaper column, the "Report Card on Education." Before retiring, Cummins served as director of state and federal funding, supervising remedial programs.

5. **Dr. James C. Dobson** hosts a daily radio program called "Focus on the Family," which is aired on 6,000 stations worldwide in more than a dozen languages. He founded this nonprofit organization in 1977. The campus in Colorado Spring is so large that it has its own zip code. Dr. James Dobson is the author of many books.

6. **Will James Durant** (1885–1981) was an American philosopher, historian, and writer. He fought for equal wages, the sufferings of women, and fair working conditions for the American labor force.

7. **Dr. Steve Farrar** is a speaker, author of many books, and the founder of Men's Leadership Ministries. He graduated from the Western Seminary, holds a master's degree, and earned a doctorate from Dallas Theological Seminary.

8. **Mahatma Gandhi** was born into a Hindu family in 1869, became a political and spiritual leader of India, and organized poor farmers and laborers to protest against oppressive taxation and discrimination. He fought against poverty, and he liberated women, moderated religious and ethnic groups, and worked on India's independence.

9. **Ernest Hemingway** was born in 1899 in Oak Park, Illinois. He drove ambulance for the Red Cross near the Italian front during WWI and established his writing skills in 1921–1926.

10. **Dr. Donald Joy** is a well-known speaker and author of many books. He has taught at Asbury Seminary since 1971 and served as a consultant to the Pentagon, the U.S. Department of Health and Human Services, and the Eli Lilly Endowment.

11. **Dr. Randy Tillman (RT) Kendall** served as pastor of the Westminster Chapel in London, England, for 25 years. Born in Ashland, Kentucky, and educated at the Southern Baptist Theological Seminary, Dr R. T. Kendall remains actively involved in writing and speaking during his retirement in Florida. He is the author of 50 books, including *Total Forgiveness.*

12. **Dr. Elisabeth Kubler-Ross** (1926–2004) earned a medical degree in Switzerland, her country of birth, and completed a degree in psychiatry at the University of Colorado. She founded Shanti Nilaya in Escondido, California, and taught about the next passage of life. She is the author of many books, of which *On Death and Dying* is well known.

13. **Karl Paul Reinhold Niebuhr** (1892–1971) was a Protestant theologian best known for his study on Christian faith in modern politics and diplomacy. Serving as pastor in Detroit he noticed the demoralizing effects of industrialism, became an outspoken critic of Henry Ford, and promoted workers' rights.

14. **Blaise Pascal** (1623–1662) was a French mathematician, physicist, and religious philosopher. His earliest works include the mechanical calculator and studies on fluids, pressure, and vacuum. His writing influenced modern economics and social science. After a mystical experience in 1654, he devoted himself to philosophy and theology. Pascal suffered from ill health throughout his life.

15. **Richard Rohr, O.F.M.** (born 1943 in Kansas) is a Franciscan priest, writer, and inspirational speaker with an open view of modern Christianity and a critical look at church hierarchy. He emphasizes community building, peace, justice, and male spirituality.

16. **Dr. Charlie Shedd** (1915–2004) was a master communicator of homespun wisdom and is the author of many books. He served as a Presbyterian minister for over 50 years and made God's truth available to the simplest folks.

17. **Charles Haddon Spurgeon** (1834–1892) was a British Baptist preacher who converted to Christianity when a snowstorm forced him to seek refuge in a chapel. Spurgeon was the most popular preacher of his day, but struggled with clinical depression.

18. **Zig Ziglar**, the tenth of twelve children, was born in Alabama. His mother raised the children herself when the father died. Ziglar served in the U.S. Navy, and became a salesman and motivational speaker.

END NOTES

Chapter 4: Impact on the Children
Deep-Rooted Fault Lines

[a] For more than 70 years, *Journal of Marriage and Family* (*JMF*) has been a leading research journal in the family field. *JMF* features original research and theory, research interpretation and reviews, and critical discussion concerning all aspects of marriage, other forms of close relationships, and families. JMF is published on behalf of the National Council on Family Relations. The web address is: http://www.ncfr.com/journals/marriage_family/home.asp.

[b] The Research Data Centres (RDC) Program is part of an initiative by Statistics Canada, the Social Sciences and Humanities Research Council (SSHRC) and university consortia to help strengthen Canada's social research capacity and to support the policy research community. RDCs provide researchers with access to microdata from population and household surveys in a secure university setting. Staffed by Statistics Canada employees, the centers operate under the provisions of the Statistics Act in accordance with all the confidentiality rules, accessible only to researchers with approved projects who have been sworn in

under the Statistics Act as "deemed employees." The web address is: http://www.statcan.gc.ca/rdc-cdr/index-eng.htm.

^c **Study: Divorce and the mental health of children** (December 2005)

According to a study from the *Research Data Centre* and published in the *Journal of Marriage and Family*, young children of parents heading for divorce tend to develop mental health problems even before a marital breakup. The study found that children whose parents eventually divorce show higher levels of depression as well as higher levels of anti-social behavior than children whose parents remain married. This survey is significant because it found that nearly one in two divorces in Canada involve dependent children.

Levels of depression and antisocial behavior were found to be higher in 1994 among the children whose parents eventually divorced. Parents who divorced by 1998 reported lower levels of marital satisfaction, and higher levels of depression and family dysfunction than when first interviewed in 1994. They also tended to be younger than the parents of families that remained intact. The study found that the same characteristics associated with parental divorce by 1998 were also associated with higher levels of childhood depression and anti-social behavior.

Once these family characteristics were taken into account, the differences in mental health at the initial interview between children whose parents divorced and children whose parents remained married were no longer detected. This suggests that it may not necessarily be divorce that is potentially damaging to child mental health. It also found that over and above these pre-existing differences, children's levels of depression tended to increase after the divorce, however, the level of anti-social behavior of children coming from highly dysfunctional families tended to decrease after the divorce.

The *National Longitudinal Survey of Children and Youth* (Cycles 1-3) provided the data to track children aged four to seven who were living with both parents in 1994. The mental health characteristics of children whose parents remained married were compared to those whose who had divorced by 1998. The analysis was conducted at the Toronto Regional Statistics Canada *Research Data Centre* at the University of

Toronto. The Research Data Centre program is part of an initiative by Statistics Canada, the Social Sciences and Humanities Research Council and University Consortia. The web address is: http://www. statcan.gc.ca/daily-quotidien/051213/dq051213c-eng.htm.

[d] Page 38. The information addressing the harmful effects of divorce is derived from the "HealingWell.com" website entitled, "Emotional Pain of Divorce Lingers Long After Split," written by Alan Mozes. For more information, visit, http://news.healingwell.com/index. php?p=news1&id=529763.

[e] Page 41. The information on child abuse was taken from a survey commissioned by the *Ontario Association of Children's Aid Society* (OACAS), funded by the Trillium Foundation. It involves 3,448 Ontarians between May 2, 2006 and June 13, 2006. The survey indicates that about half of Ontarians would be hesitant to report child abuse. More than 55 percent of people surveyed said it would be difficult to report actual or suspected cases of child abuse by someone they know well. Though many said it would be easier to report a casual acquaintance, 44 percent said they would still hesitate to make a report. According to the survey of nearly 3,500 Ontarians, the leading reason for not reporting an abuse is fear of retribution. Other reasons are not knowing where to call, a lack of understanding of what constitutes abuse and the belief that it's "not my business." More information is on "Survey reveals why Ontarians don't report child abuse" is on http://www.oacas.org/ newsroom/releases/surveyresults06oct4.pdf.

Chapter 5: Pain of Divorce
Divorce Vs. Death
[a] Page 52. The book by Elisabeth Marquardt entitled, "Between Two Worlds: The Inner Lives of Children of Divorce," chronicles a three year study which found, among other things, that many children of divorced parents experience a profound lack of trust in God and faith in the Church. Elizabeth Marquardt of the Institute for American Values and Norval Glenn, a professor of sociology at the University of Texas at Austin, co-directed the study, which was funded by the Lilly

Endowment. Marquardt and Glenn interviewed 70 young adults in the U.S. face-to-face, and compiled telephone surveys of 1,500 young adults, half of whom were raised in divorced families and half from intact families. They report that young people from divorced families "experience a loss of trust that affects their belief in God, making them overall much less religious than their peers from intact families." In addition, many of the young people raised with divorce "often say the church failed them. Of those children of divorce who were regular [attendees] at a place of worship, two-thirds say that no one from the clergy or congregation reached out when their families broke up." Most strikingly was that many children of divorced families "feel pain and loss evoked by the idea of God as a father or parent."

Marquardt and Glenn also found that for many of these children, the experience strengthened their faith. Thirtyeight percent of young people from divorced families (compared to 22 percent from intact families), say, "I think of God as the loving father or parent I never had in real life." More information is on "New study reveals spiritual effects of divorce on children," http://www.catholicnewsagency.com/new.php?n=5178.

[b] Page 53. A researcher at Ohio State University found that people who stayed married accumulated 93 percent more wealth than single or divorced people. Economist Jay Zagorsky of OSU's Center for Human Resource Research tracked the financial and marital status of more than 9,000 people from 1985 to 2000. Those who divorced saw their wealth reduced by 77 percent on average. Laura Rowly's website, "Aligning with Your Partner Financially" can be found on http://www.moneyandhappiness.com/blog/?p=156.

Chapter 9: Mental Illness in Marriage
Altered Level of Consciousness
[a] Page 95. The Surgeon General's Report on Mental Health reveals that in any given year 54 million people have a mental disorder. Shame and guilt are common by family caregivers of mentally ill people and they suffer from stresses, says Nassir Ghaemi, MD, an assistant professor of psychiatry at Harvard and director of the Bipolar Research Program at

Cambridge Hospital. Mental illness is being recognized as a biological illness and has less of a stigma now than in the past. It's no longer seen as a character defect.

The strains of mental illness on a marriage can be devastating. "There's a very high divorce rate among people who have depression or bipolar disorder," says Ghaemi. "Some spouses aren't able to take care of the other spouse when they're ill." Treatment may also cause problems and drugs like Prozac, for example, can affect a person's sexuality and feelings of desire. Ghaemi says further, "There is some evidence that being a participant in a support group is associated with doing better . . . but adds that most research is focused on family support for patients themselves and very little has been done on how family members cope and how their lives are affected."

The information is from "A Member of Your Family is Mentally Ill–What Now?" It is written by Patricia Olsen, Medical Writer and published in Dec 21, 2008. Log into the HealthyPlace, America's Mental Health Channel, http://www.healthyplace.com/bipolar-disorder/support/member-of-family-is-mentally-ill-what-now/menu-id-67/. Also check the Bipolar Disorder Center of HealthyPlace.com, http://concernedcounseling.com/Communities/Bipolar/toc.asp.

Chapter 10: Raising a Family as a Single Parent
Doing Double Duty

[a] Page 109. Information on fathers going to church as a spiritual and moral leader is published in "The Truth About Men & Church: Robbie Low on the Importance of Fathers to Churchgoing." The statistical report first appeared in 2000 and is entitled, "The Demographic Characteristics of the Linguistic and Religious Groups in Switzerland" by Werner Haug and Phillipe Warner of the Federal Statistical Office, Neuchatel. It appeared in Volume 2 of "Population Studies No. 31," as part of a book entitled "The Demographic Characteristics of National Minorities in Certain European States," published by the Council of Europe Directorate General III, Social Cohesion, Strasbourg in January 2000. The study reviews the results of a 1994 survey of Swiss religious practice and arrives at the conclusion that the impact of a father, and to a lesser extent the mother, in attending church forms an important

directive for future religious activity in the children. The study reveals that with the father attending church regularly and the mother non-practicing, 44 percent of their children became regular churchgoers. If the mother attends regularly and the father is non-practicing, only two percent of their children became regular church attendees. This shows that no matter how faithful mother's devotions is, only one child in 50 will become a regular worshipper if the father does not go to church himself. While mother's regularity may not have a long-term effect on the children attending church services, it prevents them from drifting away entirely. More information is on http://www.touchstonemag.com/archives/article.php?id=16-05-024-v.

Sharing Meals Together
[b] Page 110. There is a wealth of information concerning the subject on Sharing Meals Together. The material is derived from, "Building Strength Through Stories: Family Dinnertime Narratives" by Robyn Fivush, PhD, Emory University, Georgia. She says that, "Narratives told around the family dinner table may be especially critical for adolescents." Dr. Fivush website can be found on http://www.apa.org/pi/cyf/fam2.html. More information is available in the article "Family Meals and Disordered Eating in Adolescents" on the website "Archives of Pediatrics & Adolescent Medicine" http://archpedi.ama-assn.org/cgi/content/full/162/1/17.

Chapter 13: In the Eyes of the Children
Restitution
[a] Page 156. According to research published in the *Globe and Mail*, improving family relationships could be one way to prevent children from turning into persistent bullies.

The study led by Dr. Debra Pepler, a psychology professor at Toronto's York University, found that close to ten percent of children who bully other kids in late elementary school continue to act as bullies through high school. "These are the highest-risk youths in our society," Pepler told the *Globe and Mail*. "They haven't learned the essential lesson of how to get along with others in relationships . . . They persistently use power and aggression to control and distress others." The study concludes that behind aggression, as a news release points out, bullying children often lack a moral compass and experience a great deal of conflict in their relationships with their parents. The article, "Bullying linked to troubled families" was published on April 2 2008 by *Today's Family News* and is available on http://www.londonabc.ca/pdf/articles/2008-tfn-April2.pdf.

Chapter 14: Power of Prayers
Unfulfilled Dreams
[a] Page 168. Mary Stevenson is known to be the bona fide author of "Footprint in the Sand." She wrote the poem in 1936 after experiencing serious family tragedies. Since then, two other authors have emerged who claim copyright ownership for their own versions but with slightly changed wording. They are Margaret Fishback Powers, 1964 and Carolyn Carty, 1963. After the original text was lost and found again while moving, forensic experts granted the copyright to Mary Stevenson in 1984. The three version of "Footprint in the Sand" are on: http://www.wowzone.com/fprints.htm.

ABOUT THE AUTHOR

A native of Switzerland, Isidor immigrated to Canada to pursue a career in electronics. When the anticipated job opportunities didn't open, he pooled his savings and started his own company. In a small room in his house he worked on his inventions long into the night while raising a large family. As the business became self-sufficient, his wife became mentally ill. Even though he is a firm believer in marriage and the Christian faith, he found no other option than to divorce his wife. Misunderstandings and a rift with his Christian friends over divorce persuaded him to share the experience in this book, *God's Grace in Divorce*. Buchmann wrote the book, *Batteries in a Portable World* and published numerous articles on battery technology. He is the father of five grown children and resides in Burnaby, British Columbia, Canada.

BOOK END

Divorce can be a gift to a family . . . if it's done to save the children from a dysfunctional home. It's a shocking thesis to many readers, as it has been a troubling discovery for Isidor. He tried to fulfill God's command in marriage, but with his wife spiraling into the darkness of mental illness and the family hopelessly falling apart, he made the difficult choice to divorce. Isidor's writing conveys the passionate struggle of a man torn between strict church doctrines on one extreme and the forbidden exit on the other. The message reflects the inner turmoil of a believer who tried to follow a righteous path and got entangled in a mire of religious rules.

God's Grace in Divorce is a journey in understanding God's plan for us. It provides encouragement in knowing that we can conquer arduous times with willpower, determination, and perseverance. Accepting our destiny brings hope, healing, and inner peace. "With God, all things are possible" (Matt. 19:26).

The website **www.DivorceForJustCause.com** provides additional information about "God's Grace in Divorce." It answers questions many of us have and want to share with our friends. For personal contact, please write to Isidor Buchmann at **Buchmann@DivorceForJustCause.com**.

To order additional copies of this title call:
1-877-421-READ (7323)
or please visit our Web site at
www.winepressbooks.com

If you enjoyed this quality custom-published book,
drop by our Web site for more books and information.

www.winepressgroup.com
"Your partner in custom publishing."